Dreaming about the Divine

SUNY series in Dream Studies
Robert L. Van de Castle, editor

Dreaming about the Divine

Bonnelle Lewis Strickling

State University of New York Press

Published by
State University of New York Press, Albany

For information, address State University of New York Press,
194 Washington Avenue, Suite 305, Albany, NY 12210–2384

Production by Marilyn P. Semerad
Marketing by Michael Campochiaro

Library of Congress Cataloging-in-Publication Data

Strickling, Bonnelle Lewis, 1942–
    Dreaming about the divine / Bonnelle Strickling.
        p. cm.
    Includes bibliographical references and index.
    ISBN-13: 978–0–7914–7091–6 (hardcover : alk. paper)
    ISBN-13: 978–0–7914–7092–3 (pbk. : alk. paper)
    1. Dreams—Religious aspects. I. Title.

BL65.D67S77 2007
204'.2—dc22

2006020744

10 9 8 7 6 5 4 3 2 1

For Greg and Ladson
and with special thanks to Nancy Merritt Bell

Contents

Acknowledgments

This book would not exist without the contributions of a great many people, in particular those clients, spiritual directees, friends, and family members who were gracious enough to offer their dreams to be part of this book. Many people offered dreams that I did not have space to include, but they are still very much appreciated and they enriched my reflections. I began this project partly because I noticed how many of my clients and spiritual directees had dreams about the divine. Not only numinous once-in-a-lifetime dreams, but all sorts of dreams. I started to wonder whether this was a widespread phenomenon and I started asking people. I put a notice in our weekly church bulletin. I asked my friends. I discovered that, indeed, many people had dreams about the divine in various guises. I want to thank all the people who shared their dreams with me. It has been an honor to be trusted with them.

I also want to thank the International Association for the Study of Dreams, at whose conferences I gave many of the papers that form the basis of this book. I have consistently received helpful suggestions and feedback there that have moved my work forward, and I can't speak warmly enough about the supportive atmosphere of the IASD for the work of people engaged in dream studies. I want to particularly thank Kelly Bulkeley, who was most encouraging and supportive in the early stages of this project.

Many others were helpful to me as I worked on the book. I want to especially thank the Jung Societies of Vancouver and Victoria, British Columbia, and the Jung Society of Memphis, Tennessee. I also want to thank Dr. Bill Walker of the Counseling and Education Society of Memphis, Tennessee, who sponsored the Spirit Seminar where I presented an early version of several chapters of this book. Dr. Walker has also been personally helpful in discussions of the book. Luke Wallin was kind enough to talk about dreams, read the book, and make suggestions, and was generally very encouraging as only a teacher of creative writing could be to his old friend and former office partner from graduate school in philosophy at the University of Iowa.

As well, I especially want to thank my research assistant Janet Whyte, also a library technician at Langara College, for her exceptional work on the index. As always, Janet's sense of humor, imagination, conscientiousness and patience with my schedule has given me the kind of support with this project that every writer wants. I suspect the quality of her support is partly due to the fact that Janet is a writer herself, and a very good one.

Many things make it possible to write something close to the heart. I'd like to thank my cousin Brian Aaron and his wife Linda for my time spent in their quiet and welcoming home in Memphis, where I wrote several of the papers which formed the basis of this book. My years at the Cathedral Centre for Spiritual Direction, now alas closed, working with my directees and with my friend and colleague Shiella Fodchuk, contributed greatly. My spiritual community, Christ Church Cathedral in Vancouver, has been a continuing source of sustenance in my life, and has truly lived the motto that is posted over the front door: "Open Doors, Open Hearts, Open Minds." Perhaps what is most important is the love and support of particular people. Ladson Hinton has been a friend and mentor for many years. And most of all, not just the book but my life is unimaginable without my life's companion Greg Fuller, whose intelligence, sense of humor, and understanding are sine qua non.

Introduction

Point of View

This book is about dreams of the divine, including dreams that involve experiences of the divine and dreams whose content includes representations of the divine. While for those of us who are already interested in either dreams or the divine, the attraction of these dreams is self-evident, that's not true for everyone. So let me begin by saying what attracted me. In order to do this, I'll offer a brief sketch of my own point of view: some experience, some intellectual autobiography, and some theory.

Though I have professional interests in philosophy, psychotherapy, and religious life, these interests began as something intensely personal. As a high school student, bored with what was offered in my classes and having a strong feeling there was more to life than reading *The Scarlet Letter* and memorizing the dates of various wars, I took Plato and Nietzsche out of the public library in my small Southern town. I found myself in an unfamiliar but beckoning world. In university, I took my first philosophy course and it was love at first thought. I decided to major in philosophy because I believed it would be the pursuit of wisdom, though I had only an inkling of what that would be. Though it turned out that my professors took a somewhat different view of the study of philosophy, it was the right place for me. Training in philosophy was surprising and often overwhelming, and it helped me develop the intellectual capacities that have given me access to the work of thinkers which has been an endless source of pleasure and illumination, and a perspective which has become basic. It has been indispensable for reflecting on the central issues of life itself and my life in particular. Though I describe this in a matter-of-fact way, it's also true that things have turned out very differently than I thought they would when I was a graduate student in philosophy. My original plan was to be a full-time professional philosopher. I was in considerable conflict about the intellectual values that meant a great deal to me, and the spiritual and emotional values that I kept muffled (not just from others but from myself as well) that seemed to be rejected by the academic environment in which I spent most of my time. Being a woman and a feminist made it all even more complicated. At a certain point in graduate school, I had a major emotional crisis precipitated by divorce, and because of that crisis, I went into therapy. My therapist was very interested in dreams, and it was at this time I began a life-long-habit of recalling my dreams. Not long after I started working with her, I had the following dream:

> I am in a seminar room, leading a seminar on a topic in the philosophy of mind. Suddenly the seminar room turns into a rocket ship, turns on its end, and takes off.

I found this dream quite surprising and puzzling. Since my therapist was a Gestalt therapist, I was required to imagine myself as everything in the dream. At that point, I had a fairly limited picture of myself, so I was surprised to hear myself say, "I am a seminar room and a rocket ship." I didn't know what it meant, but somehow it seemed true. Looking back, I can see it had something to do with having things turn upside down, moving up and out, having things turn out unexpectedly, or at least differently than I thought they would, being moved towards the spiritual world, with not being exactly the career academic I was planning to be. And all those things did indeed happen. My dreams were working on me, and the divine was working through my dreams. As a result of being in therapy with that particular therapist, I began to pay a great deal of attention to my dreams.

Psychotherapy helped me create a life that belonged to me. During the time I was in therapy, I had a series of dreams with a recurring theme: I was in the dark and trying to turn on the light. This dream had various versions. Sometimes it occurred as a dream within a dream: I would turn on the light, then realize this was only a dream and I was still in the dark. Sometimes I would look for a light to turn on with no success. This contrast between being in the dark and looking for (and sometimes finding) the light has been a theme in my dreams throughout my life. It has been a strong theme in my images of the divine. I sometimes think it is one thing that has attracted me to Karl Jaspers's way of conceiving of our life's task, the elucidation of Existenz, which I will be discussing at greater length later. The implicit reference to light in the term "elucidation," which is the English translation of *Existenzhellerung* (which carries the same implicit reference in German) which I encountered in Jaspers, speaks to my own way of imagining and experiencing my search for understanding, creation, and discovery.

Psychotherapy helped me to resolve troubling emotional issues. I soon discovered Jung; the work I have done and continue to do is Jungian, and it contributed to my being able to create an authentic spiritual path that combined elements of creation, discovery, and return. It also contributed to my being able to come to see suffering as a natural part of human life, not something to be avoided or glossed over. A great deal of this has been due to work with dreams. My spiritual life has been built on my own experiences, insights, and reflections, and incorporates the whole life I have lived. Many of these insights have felt like things I have known all along, but have been unable to articulate and/or give other form to. And finally, I was able to return to the religious tradition of my childhood, having developed a very different relation to it. I realized both that I never truly understood it, and how bereft I had been in all these years I had been away from it.

In his book *The Unconscious Christian*, James Hall points out that, in our intensely secular age, there are many people who suffer from repressed spirituality in the same way that people used to be said to suffer from repressed sexuality.[1] By the same token, I believe that are many people who experience themselves as what I would call spiritual exiles, unable to return to the religious tradition in which their spiritual formation took place because the form in which they experienced it was so emotionally damaging and/or frustrating that any spiritual or religious activity felt oppressive and spiritually and emotionally dangerous. Spirituality in spiritual exiles is sometimes seen as so impossible that it is split off and repressed, denied as irrational and ridiculous, a form of emotional dependence or childishness. Sometimes there is intense spiritual longing which is felt as a deep sorrow whose source is unidentifiable. Sometimes spiritual exiles wander, puttering around the edges of other spiritual traditions that are for some reason more acceptable to them. This was my version of spiritual exile, and the tradition I puttered around the edge of was Buddhism. This was a good choice for me, because it was there I learned to meditate.[2] Jungian work allowed me to have the kind of understanding of Christianity that allowed me to return home. More about this sort of homecoming later.

From a religious standpoint, I was deeply disappointed in the Protestant Church in which I was brought up. The reasons weren't entirely clear to me, though the feelings were very strong. At the time, I thought it was because the theology I learned rejected the requirements of reason by questioning the scientific basis of evolution and believing in the literal truth of the Bible. I later realized that, though this was true, in a sense the opposite was also true: the religion I grew up with also neglected the experience of mystery and in general the importance of spiritual experience. I left church and stayed away for a very long time. Later I came to realize that, nothwithstanding all my unhappiness with it, my religious background gave me a sense of the sacred, of the importance of liturgy and corporate worship and a respect for the mysteries even if the experience of mystery was not emphasized. It pointed toward a path which, without that early religious training, I would have had much more difficulty discovering. During the time I was returning to the religion of my childhood, I had several important dreams that helped clarify my relation to it and considerably reduce my anxiety about being over-whelmed by orthodoxy. I will discuss one of those dreams later in this book. My dreams have continued to be a source of spiritual sustenance and illumination for me.

Coming into the present and intellectual life, I teach philosophy and classical studies. I have been a Jungian psychotherapist for some time. During the last fourteen years, I have added spiritual direction to my practice. My interest in the issue of the divine in all its manifestations is long-standing. My own experience has accompanied and in some instances preceded my theoretical interest. Raised in the Protestant tradition, I was moved by my first exposure to Jung, reading his autobiography, *Memories, Dreams, and Reflections*. In this book, Jung describes the contrast between his early religious upbringing and his own experience. An introspective and reflective child, he seemed to have had an attraction to the serious issues of life from the beginning: life and death, religious mystery, mystical experience. He was aware that certain topics were forbidden, that only certain parts of the personality were acceptable, and that both of his parents had depths that they did not show the world and were not even conscious of themselves. He longed for powerful experiences and at the same time was frightened by the experiences he did have. He had an early formative dream and a vision, both of which were accompanied by powerful affect. In his dream, which occurred when he was between three and four, he descended into an underground chamber in which he saw an enormous phallus sitting on a throne. He heard his mother's voice saying, "That is the man-eater."[3] Jung felt that this dream expressed the hidden underground counterpart of Jesus, the dark, buried, left-out aspect of Christianity which he spent a great deal of his intellectual life uncovering.

His vision had a similar spirit and occurred when he was twelve. One lovely summer day, he came out of school and was thinking how beautiful everything looked: the sun was shining, the sky was blue, the cathedral was beautiful. Suddenly he was gripped with terror that he was going to think something terrible, something that would condemn him to eternal damnation. For days he struggled against this terrible thought. Then finally he began to reflect on the source of this irresistible impetus to sin. Where could it come from? He ultimately concluded that it must come from God; there could be no other source. This led him to allow himself to think the terrible thought: "I gathered all my courage, as though I were about to leap forthwith into hell-fire, and let the thought come. I saw before me the cathedral, the blue sky. God sits on His golden throne, high above the world—and from under the throne an enormous turd falls upon the sparkling new roof, shatters it, and breaks the walls of the cathedral asunder."[4] Jung was profoundly relieved. He experienced having this thought as grace, as learning about true obedience to the will of the living God, as opposed to simply being "good" in the sense of following the rules as set down by scripture and tradition. On the other hand, he felt that he had a terrible secret, that he had strange experiences that others did not have, and this was a feeling that stayed with him throughout his life. In order to live his life authentically, he was required to be obedient to the living God as he experienced Him. However, this put him at odds with the tradition his father purported to support, which put him at odds with his father. This was a position he found himself in many times in many ways throughout his life.

Reading about Jung's life, I felt both affirmation and envy: Affirmation of my own longing for spiritual experience and the sense that spiritual experience is an essential part of life. Affirmation of my own profound boredom with a great deal of what was presented at church and the way it was taught. How I identified with Jung's disappointment in the nontransformative quality of his confirmation! I felt envy of Jung's capacity for authenticity and tolerance of unusual experience, beginning even in childhood, and envy of his courage and ability to explore his own experience in solitude. Though later I came to see that these capacities of Jung's expressed a degree of emotional disturbance as well as spiritual gift, nevertheless I continued to feel that he had access to levels of experience that many of us feel separated from or are too frightened to explore. When I studied Jung, I had a sense of recognition of something that I had always known, particularly his view that inner work involves an ongoing sense of connection with the transcendent. Jung's view that spiritual life is a natural aspect of human life, that the psyche has a drive towards creativity and spiritual experience, seemed self-evidently true to me and filled me with relief after one too many encounters with the spiritual options of atheism or rigid externalized religion.

In my philosophical life,[5] my interest in Continental philosophy led me to Karl Jaspers. Jaspers sees our innate desire to understand and live out what it is to be that extraordinary phenomenon, an existing human being as "elucidating Existence." "Elucidation" here has to do with both understanding (though not entirely intellectually) the nature of our being and living out our possibilities. Jaspers' views are in many ways similar to Jung's, including his notion of "reading ciphers," his way of describing the symbolic life. Of particular interest to me has been Jaspers's discussion of what he calls "boundary situations," basic situations in human life that both limit and define us. I will discuss these at greater length below. His emphasis on process, reflectiveness, and intellectual/intuitive activity that is connected to one's own vital questions seems close to Jung's emphasis on consciousness and meaning. His view of communication both between human beings and within oneself as essential to the authentic life is akin to Jung's view of the importance of relationship in self-knowledge and the fundamental activity of making the unconscious conscious. Both of these thinkers offer us a picture of what constitutes a meaningful and satisfying human life that involves experience of our own depths, recognizing the realities of human experience including its limitations, finding a way of life and being that we experience as meaningful, and being in relation to the transcendent in some form. If we take Jung and Jaspers seriously, we are forced to come to some disturbing conclusions about the quality of human life in the contemporary world. Many people experience their lives as an endless series of tasks, reject whatever religious upbringing they might have had, often for what they feel are excellent reasons, and feel at a loss as to how to change the quality of their lives. This brings us to another useful philosopher.

In *Being and Time*, Martin Heidegger describes human beings as Dasein, the beings who are interested in being. Not being in the abstract, but our own being, what it is to be a human being. At the same time, Heidegger believes that we have a strong tendency to forget being. What Heidegger seems to mean by this is that we become distracted from our own natures through the way our identities are formed. Heidegger believes that we develop our identities through seeing ourselves in the eyes of others. This means that we come to see both ourselves and human life in terms of an externally defined identity. This externally defined identity is not limited to, putting it in psychological terms, taking on the projections of another person. Rather, Heidegger envisions that process as producing a kind of group identity, which he calls *das Man*, "the They." This "They" identity blocks self-awareness, which Heidegger thinks of as interest in both the nature of one's own being and in creating an autonomous sense of self. Heidegger sees the authentic task of Dasein as both discovery and creation: the discovery of the nature of Dasein, and the creation of an individual and authentic life. There is an overlap here between Heidegger's views and Jung's view, as expressed in Jung's paper "The Transcendent Function," that the demands of modern life require such continuous conscious attention that a thick wall is created between the conscious and the unconscious so that the demands and activities of the unconscious will not distract the conscious mind from its task of survival in the modern world. This leads us to being cut off from the unconscious, forgetting our deeper being. This is additional to the collective identity in which Jung believes we all participate unconsciously. Jung believed that work with dreams is particularly effective in stirring up the unconscious so that it can penetrate both collective identity and the barrier between conscious and unconscious, revealing our own depths to us. Heidegger does not have the notion of the unconscious, but he does believe that there are authentic possibilities of Dasein that are hidden from us through our identification with the They, and can be revealed through our moods, particularly the angst associated with knowledge of our own death. This is not conscious knowledge, but reveals itself through feeling; feeling precedes conscious knowledge of its cause. Thus for Heidegger as well as Jung, a deeper force must penetrate our unconsciousness, an unconsciousness that is both created and reinforced by having a socially based identity: "the They" in Heidegger's case, and the collective in Jung's.

Given all this, it is important that we consciously seek out ways to have a sense of connection with our own depths. What is at issue is, for both Heidegger and Jung, an authentic life, and for Jung a connection with the transcendent. Given the degree of blockage proposed by Heidegger and Jung, this is not a simple matter. We need a source that is accessible and generally available. Work on dreams is one of the most accessible, engaging, and theologically nonthreatening ways for people to cultivate self-knowledge and the capacity for depth, and to develop an authentic relation to the divine. A vital spiritual life is, ultimately, based on spiritual experience of one's own. The capacity for spiritual experience seems universal, yet for many it seems elusive and remote. Dreams offer us an open door, a way of being in relation to ourselves that leads to a lifetime of enriching and enriched experience.

Finally, both doing my own work and working with clients in spiritual direction, I noticed how often dreams came forward in periods of spiritual confusion, crisis, and struggle, presenting people with images of the divine that were completely unexpected yet very much what was needed at that moment. Dreams helped people both in spiritual formation, when they were seeking a spiritual path, and in spiritual direction, when they had decided on a spiritual path and sought to deepen their relation to it. These personal experiences and experiences with clients emphasized to me the creative and unlimited quality of the divine, and the importance of not becoming unduly attached to a particular image of the divine. It seems clear that this was the reason that Jung was so suspicious of organized religion and the tendency that people have to be spiritually lazy in the sense that they allow institutionalized religious practice to substitute for their own experience. I will discuss our relation to institutionalized religion at some length later on, but one aspect of our relation to religious tradition is one that demands continuing attention: if we do not have a living relation to our own inner spiritual sources we will not have a spiritual life. A vibrant spiritual life is based on personal spiritual experience; attention to and work with dreams is a rich source of that experience. A substantial part of this book is devoted to discussion of these experiences.

All of these ways of looking at the world, philosophical, psychological and spiritual, have been important in my understanding of life, and dreams have been relevant in developing each point of view. Dreams can be an instrument in our struggle towards authenticity and resistance of shallowness, or what the existentialists would call inauthenticity or bad faith, which in turn can enable us to stay in contact with our deeper selves and sustain a relation to the divine in all its manifestations, which in turn allows us to understand more of the possibilities of being, in both the individual and transcendent senses, than we might ever have imagined.

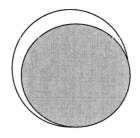

1

The Divine

This book is about dreams about the divine. However, thus far, I have discussed only the importance of our experience of depth, the areas of life that offer us particular challenges, and some theories of human nature offered by Jung, Jaspers, and Heidegger that describe the complexity of human beings and our tendency to stay on the surface of life rather than living deeply. I haven't yet talked about what seems the central concept in a book about dreams about the divine: what is meant here by "the divine"?

The short answer to this question is "whatever you think it means." When I collected material for the book I asked people to contribute dreams that they believed were about the divine. The result was material in two basic categories: dreams that had a special "feel," what Jung would call numinous dreams, and dreams whose subject matter was identified by the dreamers as having to do with the divine. Thus dreams in the former category are identified by a certain quality of experience, while dreams in the latter are identified by subject matter. Some dreams combine these qualities, for example, numinous dreams about recognizable religious figures such as Jesus. From my point of view as a therapist and spiritual director, many of these dreams also marked important changes in the points of view or lives of the dreamers. In some instances, they provided insight, healing, and hope. In others, they were deeply disturbing and frightening, leaving the dreamers with a sense of contact with a threatening otherness.

After a famous interview on the BBC in which he said he did not *believe* in God, but rather *knew*, Jung replied to the many letters received by the BBC in a letter to *The Listener* on January 21, 1960. In his letter, he describes God in the following way: "This is the name by which I designate all things

which cross my willful path violently and recklessly, all things which upset
my subjective views, plans and intentions and change the course of my life for
better or worse. In accordance with tradition I call the power of fate in this
positive as well as negative aspect, and inasmuch as its origin is beyond my
control, 'god', a 'personal god', since my fate means very much myself, particularly when it approaches me in the form of conscience as a vox Dei, with
which I can even converse and argue. (We do and, at the same time, we
know that we do. One is subject as well as object.)"[1] One way and another,
all these dreams crossed the paths of and changed the dreamers: dreamers who
were deeply unhappy felt healed and comforted, dreamers who were compla-
cent or stuck were disturbed, dreamers who were searching and wondering
about meaning were illuminated. Contact with the divine changes people,
and perhaps this is one of most reliable indicators of the presence of the
divine: something comes into consciousness and makes a change that is not
driven by will, that is unexpected and spontaneous. This leaves aside questions about the nature of the divine. Dreamers have experienced the divine as
the Christian God, as a Canadian mountie, as a terrifying force, as a magical
animal. Traditional concepts of the divine in all the major religious traditions
allow for the possibility of many representations of the divine, including radical nonrepresentation, such as the Buddhist notion of the divine as nothing,
no-thing, or the experience of the divine as overwhelming noncognitive
affect, such the experience of Bruder Klaus as discussed by Jung.[2]
Contemporary psychoanalysts such as Bion and Lacan talk about "O" and
"jouissance".[3] Nothing can be excluded. Jaspers sees all ways of envisioning
the divine as incomplete; in his view, Transcendence is ultimately indefinable,
and what we envision and experience is a representation of Transcendence
that points to the transcendent realm but is by no means complete or
absolute. Each way of experiencing and/or conceiving of the divine is what
he calls a cipher, and our relation to these ciphers is an aspect of the elucidation of Existenz, which he sees as a gift from the Transcendent. This is a particularly important point, since virtually all the dreamers represented here
experience these images as important factors in their own relation to the
divine, whether the divine is experienced in a person-to-person relationship
or as a more overwhelming and impersonal presence. The possibility of spiritual depth seems to depend to a great extent on the ability of individuals to
have and accept what they would identify as living, personal spiritual experience, which can and indeed ought to be quite idiosyncratic. This means that
we must include all sorts of experiences of the divine, not just the familiar or
the pleasant.

This also leaves aside the question of actions on the basis of experiences
of the divine. It is not, unfortunately, unfamiliar to hear of people who
murder others because "God told them to." Are these people having experi-

ences of the divine? From a Jungian standpoint, these experiences are genuinely archetypal, but they are unassimilable because they are not mediated
by the ego. From a traditional Christian standpoint, they would be seen as
experiences of the demonic, which is in its own way transcendent, though
not ultimate. However, in both instances there is a sense of consciousness
being overwhelmed by the negative divine, with no apparent possibility for
conscious choice or reflection. For the divine to work constructively in our
lives, we need to be able to come into conscious relation with it in some
way other than being driven by it. And again, this is furthered by our
accepting our own experiences as genuine rather than denying them, no
matter how unlikely they may seem. Accepting them as genuine can include
finding them repellent and frightening, and refusing to act on them, as well
as being inspired and delighted.

Why This, Why Here, Why Now?

So far, I have presented dreams about the divine in both a Jungian and
a more generally spiritual framework. From these points of view, we could
say that dreams about the divine have their origins in the Self and the tendency of archetypes to incarnate. From the spiritual standpoint, we can talk
about the longing for the divine, the sense that there is a spark of the divine
in ourselves that calls out to the transpersonal divine, or we could say the
divine seeks us through the unconscious. A sense of its presence in waking
life is often considerably enhanced by dreams about the divine. Dreams
about the divine often occur when we are in life situations that we want to
change but can't see any way to change, the kind of situation that often
involves suffering, frustration, grief, severe disappointment, and/or loss.
These are the existential conditions that characterize both life and ourselves,
conditions that we experience as limitations, but that could also be
described as structuring our possibilities.

I have arranged the dreams we will examine in two ways. First, I have
created three categories: dreams of comfort, healing, and renewal, dreams of
energy, and "bad" dreams. These categories are not exhaustive, but they represent three fundamental ways in which we can experience the divine in the
psyche. Dreams of comfort, healing, and renewal are generally related to situations in which there has been psychic wounding of various kinds; the wound
in the psyche is not just soothed but to some degree healed through the
dream. Dreams of energy often occur in situations in which severe limitation
is experienced and there is apparently unresolvable conflict about what to do:
they contain unexpected, often frightening, inrushes of numinous psychic
energy. "Bad" dreams can also be related to limitation, unresolved conflict,

and dangerous unconsciousness: these are dreams that are frightening, disturbing, and often painful, but at the same time seem to concern one's life beyond the purely personal.

Second, I will offer two case studies, work with clients in which dreams about the divine were especially important. One of these case studies is an illustration of the extraordinary part played by changing relations with the divine through a client's lifetime.

I will also discuss the presence of dreams about the divine in transference and countertransference, and the role they can play for both client and therapist/spiritual director.

All of these dreams can be seen as responses to what Jaspers refers to as boundary situations.[4] In Jaspers's view, human life contains kinds of situations that are inevitable, in that, whatever the content of our experience, it will be structured in these ways. One of the tasks of the authentic human being is to come into relation with these situations in some way other than experiencing them unreflectively (which often leads to feeling victimized by them) or knowing about them theoretically. For Jaspers it is important for us to confront them, to come into some kind of conscious relation to them as structuring the possibilities of our lives. Boundary situations are both limiting and delineate possibilities: we cannot avoid them, but they create occasions for consciousness, choice, and possible increase of depth. Jaspers's boundary situations are both general and particular. There is the historicity of existential existence and the dubiousness of existential existence. In particular, there are death, suffering, struggle, and guilt. In my own view, we can add to these particular boundary situations two more, which are related: disappointment and loss.

Describing boundary situations briefly we can say the following. In general, we cannot avoid living in a particular time in history with particular parents in a particular place. We also cannot avoid the contingency of human existence, the fact that any resolution we might find to a particular problem of existence is finite, and that this situation is unchangeable. These are conditions of our existence in the world. In particular, we cannot avoid either death or the knowledge of our own deaths. We cannot avoid suffering: we inevitably experience suffering, and we cannot avoid seeing the universality of human suffering, often great human suffering. Struggle too is a basic feature of human existence, since resources are limited. As well, we struggle for understanding with other human minds, and we struggle through love to truly understand another human being, thereby understanding ourselves as well. Guilt is inevitable because we have both possibilities and are required to choose among them. We are responsible for both what we choose and what is rejected, and this responsibility is cumulative in that we create ourselves through a lifetime of choice, and are responsible for this creation: the choices define us and limit us, and our guilt is a result of this responsibility and these choices. Finally, no matter how successful we are, no matter how our lives flourish, we cannot help experiencing disappointment and loss. We have dreams and fantasies that are never fulfilled, often dreams and fantasies that are crucially important to the meaning of our lives. Our personal relations invariably involve some degree of disappointment, sometimes quite severe disappointment. Things often, perhaps always, turn out much differently than we thought or hoped they were going to. Loss too is a basic feature of human life. as the Roman Stoics point out, ultimately everything is lost, and in the meantime, everything is contingent and fragile. People and other beings we love age and die, we lose sources of emotional security through social change and displacement, we lose money and resources.

We can relate to all these situations in a number of ways: resentment, avoidance, knowledge without application to ourselves, and entering into them as belonging to us and generating possibilities for authenticity. This last way leads us to consciousness and authentic actions through which we bring more of our being into the world and live from our depths. Jaspers distinguishes between the aspects of human being that can be described empirically and objectively through the sciences, and that which is essentially subjective and indescribable. "Jaspers calls this non-empirical dimension of humanity 'Existenz,' that is the nonobjective actuality of self-being, true self-hood, existential freedom, undetermined moral decision, or the genuine and authentic self."5 Our central task, which goes beyond empirical understanding and intellectual activity, is the continuous, self-aware, and creative living out of Existenz which Jaspers calls "the elucidation of Existenz."

One of the main challenges of the elucidation of Existenz is the challenge of self-knowledge. Not theoretical self-knowledge, but intimate self-knowledge. Jaspers believes this is achieved to a great extent through the communication that goes on in authentic relationships. Jaspers envisions some of the most important self-knowledge as emerging from "the loving struggle for Existenz," a way of living out the boundary situation of struggle that can be creative for both people involved. Both people are committed to speaking the truth as each knows it and being willing to challenge and be challenged undefensively in their common commitment to the development of Existenz in each. This image of the struggle to manifest as yet unknown depths is highly relevant to both inner work and work with dreams.

Deep inner work, whether through spiritual direction or therapy/analysis, can be seen as a version of the loving struggle for Existenz. Both people involved are committed to self-knowledge, both want to speak the truth, to challenge, and be challenged. It differs from Jaspers's description in that the relation is not a relation between equals in the sense that the spiritual director or therapist/analyst is sought out because the client believes she or he can help. Thus there is the issue of transference and countertransference, based on the asymmetries of experienced authority or power. Nevertheless, the experience of spiritual direction or therapy/analysis that enables one to discover oneself at a deep level looks and feels very much like the struggle described by Jaspers.

Self-knowledge can also result from the struggle with Existenz in which one struggles with oneself. Jaspers describes this as the part of the process of self-becoming. "But struggle is not just an interrelation of human beings; it goes on in the individual as well. Existenz is the process of *self-becoming*, which is *a struggle with myself*. I stunt possibilities that are inherent in me and coerce my impulses; I shape my given propensities, question what I have become, and am aware of being only when I do not recognize my being as something I own."[6]

Jaspers's paradigm seems to be the struggle of two individuals. It is the fearless communication elicited in this struggle that helps us discover ourselves and others, the challenge to our persistent tendency to self-deception and avoidance that loving struggle helps overcome. His discussion of the inner struggle is extremely brief. However, thinking in terms of depth psychology, we can see how this sort of challenge and struggle between conscious and unconscious, and between ego and Self can apply to the inner life. These struggles require the same self-respect and compassion for one's own suffering that the person-to-person struggle requires of one for another.

One of the most compelling reasons for my connecting Jaspers with Jung is the part that communication plays in the elucidation of Existenz. The point of work with dreams is communication between the conscious and the unconscious and in dreams about the divine, between the Self and the ego. This relationship is ongoing and never ending in both the Jungian process of individuation and in Jaspers's picture of the elucidation of Existenz. We speak to ourselves, we speak to others, and others speak to us as truthfully as possible, and through this discourse we achieve depth of understanding, an expanded sense of ourselves, more intimate relations with ourselves, others, and the divine. Jung's unconscious enriches Jaspers's picture of the elucidation of Existenz, and Jaspers's concept of boundary situations and his detailed analyses of our existential situation enriches Jung's notion of the structure of the psyche.[7]

One reason the image of struggle is both appealing and helpful for inner work is phenomenological. We have all read case studies of people who do deep and painful work. Often the pain is well described, but the ongoing sense of struggle is not. To commit oneself to inner work is to commit oneself to a great deal of uncertainty and turbulence, living in conflict without forcing resolution, and experiencing profound ambivalence about what is emerging before, during, and after. Freud's essay "The Uncanny"[8] gives us a sense of how difficult it often is to tolerate the feelings that surround the emergence of distressing repressed material. This leads inevitably to a great deal of ambivalence about the process itself. I have often had clients who were in the midst of painful work say, " I didn't want to come today," and mean it. Clients forget, are late, get lost on the way, have to cancel because of suddenly arising work commitments. All this can be connected with this ambivalence. The more powerful and significant the material that is trying to emerge, the greater the ambivalence and anxiety. Given these difficulties, the tenacity of clients is surprising. What helps them persist in the struggle?

One of the chief factors is a growing sense of connection with one's deeper self. There is something indescribably satisfying about the sense of discovery and recognition of our own inner depths, the recovery of parts of ourselves that have been split off and abandoned. We can find that we know ourselves for the first time, and at the same time that we knew all along we were there, but had lost ourselves. There is also the extraordinary satisfaction of inner contact with the divine. It brings spirituality inside and gives a sense of the personal nature of spiritual work as opposed to the institutional quality of spiritual life that so many have grown up with. I use the term "satisfaction" rather than "pleasure," because satisfaction of desire differs in quality from pleasure. There are many opportunities for pleasure in life, and they often give rise to many others. Experiencing pleasure is not the end of anything. But the satisfaction of desire puts an end to the desire because the longing or yearning has been fulfilled. Desire is replaced not by satiation but by satisfaction.[9] One way we can come to discover what our deepest needs are is through the sometimes unlooked for sense of satisfaction. It seems odd to talk about discovering our deepest needs; surely if they are so deep, we should know what they are. However, as Heidegger has pointed out, we have a propensity to forget ourselves, to forget, as he would say, Being. We need to be reminded. Heidegger thought angst would remind us of our most pressing possibility, death. But there are other possibilities and other reminders. A deep and sometimes unlooked for sense of satisfaction can be one of them. The deeper the satisfaction, the more important the desire. Doing inner work, people often experience the deepest satisfaction of their lives, a level of satisfaction they hadn't thought possible. Satisfaction, relief, insight, are all marks of satisfying our deepest desires.

As we will see, a great deal of the dream activity in each chapter is engendered by our relation to boundary situations. Boundary situations combine with the demands of the psyche for development to produce situations in which the boundaries are sharply experienced. This is often frustrating and conflictual. It can also be stimulating and fruitful. One of the main difficulties of boundary situations is that they require us to understand them in a new way, and doing that requires the release of unconscious energy. In the most radical instances of increased understanding, the energy that comes from the unconscious is divine energy, potentially bringing healing and a new point of view. Dreams about the divine offer us access to the energy in one of the least threatening ways possible. Dreams about the divine feel far less frightening than, for example, the appearance of a strange figure at the foot of one's bed at 5:00 A.M.. Dreams about the divine are often transitional: they assist in a change of viewpoint in a way that may be disturbing, but is also satisfying. They can be disturbing because they are a particularly intense version of the dream world as the world of the other in which we need to be open to meaning being given in an entirely different way, satisfying because they speak to our deep desire, often forgotten, to be in relation to our whole beings and to Being itself.

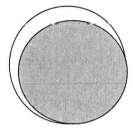

2
Some Basic Considerations

Contemporary human life is stressful and demanding. As a result, we tend to be focused on what's right in front of us. This usually means that we are focused on work, on family, on getting things done. These days, people are often so exhausted at the end of the day that, when they stop getting things done, they are unable do anything but go to bed. Yet most of us would admit to a longing for more meaning in life. Part of that meaning for many people is having a better relation with themselves. And to understand what would constitute a better relation to ourselves, we need to think more carefully about who we are.

To be a human being is to have a human nature. What that human nature might be has been a subject of debate throughout human history and across many branches of knowledge. Religion, philosophy, anthropology, sociology, biology all have their versions of what it is to be a human being. My focus in this book is on human nature in the sense of the human experience of ourselves in the world. We tend to pay more attention to certain aspects of our experience than others, yet those aspects that are neglected or ignored often have the most potential for enriching and deepening our understanding of what kind of beings we are, who we are as individuals, and how we can live these human lives most fully and authentically.

Creation and Discovery

One of the central tasks of a fully and deeply lived human life is to become what it is in us to be. This is a task of both creation and discovery. It is creation in the sense that we have, as Simone de Beauvoir has said, an open future.[1] This is a view characteristic of existentialism: the future is possibility, not yet determined, and, in the light of this, we have choices about what we do and who we become. In this sense, we are able to create ourselves and our lives. However, the existentialists do not include in their analysis of the human self the presence of depths which are unavailable to direct conscious experience and which have a powerful effect on, perhaps are even the source of, who we are. There are a range of these kinds of views. To go to the other end of the history of Western philosophy, where the individual has far less responsibility for creating self and meaning, Plato and Aristotle would both have argued (though from different points of view) that when we are born, we are someone already. Plato would have argued that we are someone in the sense that we have access to another level and kind of being through the knowledge we once had as disembodied souls in the ideal realm.[2] We are not simply blank slates, soaking up information. Rather, through reason and reflection we can remember what we once knew and thus discover the reality that underlies and transcends the realities of everyday experience. In this sense, we have an epistemic identity: we are potential knowers, and knowledge is the source of our experience of meaning and depth. When Socrates talked about the unexamined life as not being worth living, he meant that unexamined assumptions are not worthy of being called knowledge and not worthy of being the basis of our understanding of the meaning of human life. Aristotle would have argued that we come equipped with an essence which determines the kinds of beings we are, and in order to live well we must know who we are and consciously live in a way that allows this essence to develop to its fullest capacity. For Aristotle, this meant the fullest possible development of our rational and reflective capacities. The test of this development is the presence of the kind of character that allows us to choose the mean in situations that have moral significance. The virtues that characterize the mean are virtues such as courage, generosity, self-possession, pride, truthfulness, and temperance. From an Aristotelian point of view, we already have an identity as rational beings, capable of participating in human life in virtuous ways. Like Plato, our identity is tied to our capacities as thinkers and knowers. Plato and Aristotle also believe we have individual identities, and these identities are tied to our talents and abilities. So we have dual identities as both knowers and doers. Our identities as knowers are the shared human identity. Our identities as doers are as individual as our abilities. Both Plato and Aristotle place emphasis on the development of skills as basic to individual identity.

This notion of given identity as having to do with what we are able to know is a prominent theme in the Western philosophical tradition, and there are many variations on it. In the Christian tradition, we are identified as not only knowers of God but also as being known by God (see, for example,

Augustine's many passionate descriptions of both knowing and being known by God).³ It is a crucial part of who we are that God takes an interest in us as individuals, that we can open ourselves to God in prayer, that this will have an effect on how we live our individual lives. At the same time, our task is to transcend our individual identities in the sense of our individual desires, seen as prideful (see Augustine) thus sinful, and to replace our own wills with the will of God. God has given us free will, but we must use it to choose God rather than ourselves.

The emphasis on will ultimately brings us to existentialism through Kant and his emphasis on autonomy in the moral life. For Kant, we already have an identity as knowers both in the purely epistemic sense and in the moral sense. Epistemically, we come equipped with a certain set of categories which determine our experience of the world. Morally we come equipped with a rational will, which commands us to apply the categorical imperative. In the end, for Heidegger and Sartre, the moral imperative falls away, and we are left with our identities as certain kinds of beings. For Heidegger, we are the beings who are interested in being; as it turns out, it is our own being in which we are interested, not being in general. We have facticity, that which we cannot change, and Existenz, our possibilities. Our fixed capacities are a combination of our past and the structure of our being. Our possibilities are the various ways in which we can come into relation with our past and know our being. For Heidegger, our "ownmost possibility" is the way in which we come into relation with and live out the knowledge of our own deaths. Simone de Beauvoir, with whom we began this summary, argues that possibility itself, an "open future" is our most important existential feature and our efforts ought to be directed towards the exploration and commitment that turn possibility into an actuality authentically chosen.⁴

In contrast to the existentialists, but as a result of the same tradition of concerns, psychoanalysis and depth psychology have given us the picture of human beings as constituted by both a conscious and unconscious mind. In both Freudian and Jungian psychology, the conscious mind has considerably less to do with who we are than the unconscious mind. In this sense, we have a complex given identity as the possessors of, from a Freudian standpoint, drives and structures for both satisfying and transforming these drives, and, from a Jungian standpoint, as possessors of an unconscious filled with complexes whose nature is determined by archetypal energies, driven by a kind of psychic energy which moves us towards both the satisfaction of desire and the experience of meaning. For both Freud and Jung, the quality of our lives is determined by how we consciously come into relation with these pervasive and structuring unconscious activities.

All of these conceptions of human identity as at least partially fixed include experiential identity and objectively observable identity. We both experience ourselves in certain ways and can be observed to have certain qualities. In the instances of a fixed identity that is essentially connected to the divine, such as Plato's notion of the Good or the Christian notion of God, an important aspect of who we are lies in our inherent ability to experience the divine. In Plato, this is characterized as a kind of knowing that enables us to have a deep understanding of, and a profound experience of the meaning of, reality itself. In the Christian tradition, it is knowing in a different sense, in that we can have direct experience of God and the love of God that is more like our experience of human relationship than an essentially epistemic relation. Thus part of our fixed identity is who we experience ourselves as being. Plato also thought the nature of our being was objectively observable through the use of rational discourse and argument. For example, Socrates demonstrated in *Meno* that a slave boy, if asked the right questions, could demonstrate the capacity to recall his innate knowledge of geometry. Aristotle believed we could both experience our own capacities as rational beings capable of the development of virtue, and that our status as beings with essences was objectively observable both from the standpoint of watching human behavior (including the human capacity for exercising reason) and from the point of view of our place in a natural world constituted by beings who also had various essences. The same can be said for Kant and the existentialists. However, both Heidegger and Sartre introduced the notion of self-deception as a feature of what it is to be a human being that makes our experience of our identity more complex. Heidegger referred to it as forgetting being, and Sartre as bad faith. In both instances, it can be true to say that we have an identity but we may not be consciously aware of what it is. Thus becoming who we are becomes at least partially a project of discovery, not of some ultimate reality as Plato would have held, but of some deeper and perhaps more basic part of ourselves. And if this is true for Heidegger and Sartre, it is even more significant for Freud and Jung. Psychoanalysis and depth psychology both offer us the picture of ourselves as hidden from ourselves. We believe we are who we experience ourselves consciously as being, but inevitably we are deceived; indeed, often we must be deceived to be able to endure the conditions of social life. From a Jungian standpoint, we fail to grasp not only the contents of our repressed complexes, but also the extent to which our identity and fate are determined by archetypal energies. From these points of view, our identities are so hidden that we require the assistance of an analyst to help us discover who we truly are and to come into a more satisfying relation with this underlying reality.

Examining these various points of view, it can be seen that there are aspects of our lives that are accessible to our wills and aspects that are not. Those aspects that are accessible to our wills are amenable to choice and can be areas of conscious creation. Those that are not must first be discovered and related to in some way. While they may not be accessible to our wills, our knowledge and acceptance of them are essential to our experience of ourselves as whole beings. Let us examine the importance of this difference in a slightly different way.

The Voluntary and the Involuntary

Human life is a rich mixture of experience of those events and activities which are in our control, and those events and experiences that are not: the voluntary and the involuntary,[5] the internally determined and the externally determined. The voluntary and the internally determined include whatever is accessible to will and choice in both the short and long terms. This includes both the activities of reason and reason-based choice, as well as those choices that are made from other sources, such as emotion. The involuntary includes what happens *in* us spontaneously: desire, emotion, dreams, visions, mystical experience. The externally determined includes what happens *to* us: other people's actions, events in the natural world, large social events such as war.

In the Western philosophical tradition, there is a long history of focus on what is rational and what is accessible to the will and its relation to the irrational, the involuntary, and the externally determined. As we have seen above, Aristotle's notion of virtue offers us a picture of moral life in which it is possible, through consciousness, will, education, and self-discipline, to shape our own moral development and become virtuous. Though the fact that human beings have the nature they do is not in our control, our relation to it is, at least to a large extent. Aristotle included in character our emotional attitudes to the things that happen in our lives. Achieving the Golden Mean is partly a matter of which actions we choose, but also a matter of the kind of attitudes we have. To be virtuous is to be a certain kind of person, which includes not only actions but also emotions and attitudes. Aristotle did not envision emotions and attitudes as entirely reactive; he believed certain emotions and attitudes can be cultivated. The presence of emotion itself is involuntary since it is an aspect of human experience, but the quality of emotional response is the result of the cultivation of character. The Roman Stoics offer us a different but related way of dealing with the fact that much in life cannot be controlled. They advocate detachment and calm self-possession. In Epictetus's work *Enchiridion*, one of his first pieces of moral advice is: know what you can control and what you can't.[6] Marcus Aurelius recommends that we cultivate an indifference to whether our lives are long or short. Seneca recommends the development of serenity through the simple life and the discipline of desire. All of these philosophers are addressing themselves to the fact that the involuntary and the externally determined play an important part in our lives and we must find a way to be in relation to this fundamental feature of existence.

Another area in which these relationships are examined is the theory and practice of psychoanalysis. Analytic theories, both Freudian and Jungian, offer a picture of human beings as composed of the experience of consciousness and the belief that the choices we make are based on evidence and reason, and at the same time energies that are not conscious yet determine not only choices, but our sense of what is significant and meaningful. The activity of analysis is a way of engaging with these involuntary energies, and is in a sense training for conducting our own inner lives in such a way that the conscious comes into some kind of relation with the unconscious.

Using different terminology, the same thing can be said of religion and spiritual practice. All the major religious traditions presuppose that human life is embedded in and surrounded by forces and/or beings that are other and that at the same time have a great deal of power in human life. There are a number of versions of this view. As an example, Christianity offers us a model of an extremely intimate relationship between the divine and human beings. Not only does the divine determine the nature of the universe, the divine also loves each of us personally. This is both heartening and terrifying. In the Christian universe we are closer to the Other than we are to our fellow human beings. God is present in us, loves us, and wants us to live a certain way (though wanting here is obviously an attempt to characterize a mysterious relationship in human terms). At the other end of the intimacy spectrum, Buddhism offers a picture of the divine as non-Being, indescribable, certainly not anything with which we could be in relation. Our task is to free ourselves of illusory differences from the One and rejoin it. There are of course many other versions of this relationship. But in each version, there are spiritual practices that are focused on using the will and even reason to approach a relation with the divine, which appears in experience in its own time. There is no direct relation between spiritual practice and experience of the divine; spiritual practice seems to set the stage, so to speak, for experience of the divine. It turns our attention away from the world towards the divine. It makes a space for contact with the divine. Nevertheless, sometimes people experience spontaneous manifestations of the divine without any spiritual practice at all, and others may practice for years without such experience, or find it only after a very long time. Buddhism is filled with stories of people who have practiced meditation for years and finally experience enlightenment at some unlikely time, perhaps it even wakens the person from sleep. Spiritual practice may set the stage for the divine, but it manifests on its own schedule.

It is imperative in human life that we develop a relation to the involuntary and the externally determined. First of all, if we do not, we will be ignoring a substantial aspect of human life. Both our experience of the external world and our experience of ourselves is saturated with the involuntary and the externally determined. It is perhaps easier to find a relation to the externally determined than the involuntary. Life is constantly delivering events to us that we must respond to, and we are accustomed to experiencing and meeting these demands. Our relation to the involuntary is more complex. For example, many people are not aware of the extent to which involuntary emotional response determines the way they cope with the externally determined. We become accustomed to being ourselves, and come to believe that our responses are based exclusively on reflection and choice. Many people manage to focus so exclusively on everyday activity that their emotions become suppressed and they do not notice the inner processes that are constantly taking place. Furthermore, many people are frightened by unexpected inner events. This is often described as a fear of "going crazy." In my experience with clients in psychotherapy and spiritual direction, both strong emotion and the experience of the divine are often greatly feared as resulting in fragmentation of the personality ("I won't be myself anymore"), emotional possession ("If I start crying I'll never stop"), uncontrollable impulses ("If I really get angry I don't know what I'll do"), and being overwhelmed by the divine ("There won't be any of me left").[7] Given our culture, this is not surprising. We are encouraged to be goal oriented and outwardly focused. We are encouraged to believe that if we try hard enough, we can have whatever we want. A strong sense of agency is highly valued. In a sense, we are addicted to both the activities of the will and the illusion that this kind of activity is what constitutes and ought to constitute the bulk of human life activities and experience. As in the case of any addiction, the first step to loosening its grip is the acknowledgment of its existence.

This means we need to face the fact that human beings are complex and multilayered. Though our everyday lives are filled with conscious activity and require an almost constant attention to the many tasks that fill them, there is as much or more activity taking place at an unconscious level. The fact that conscious life receives our full attention contributes to the illusion connected with conscious life that our lives are under control, and failures of control are exceptional. This illusion has the advantage of giving us a sense of greater security in our lives and lowers our anxiety levels as long as it goes unchallenged. It has the disadvantage of being false. Challenges to our illusory sense of control, such as personal and family losses and tragedies, often result in the forced relinquishing of this illusion. Very often, when people are put in this position they go through a long period of feeling lost and depressed. Their sense of meaning is lost. During such periods, people can become more open to the notion that life is more than our conscious, purpose-directed experience of it. Great grief is often accompanied by a kind of inner quiet, giving us the opportunity to notice our own inner life. It is often during periods of grief and other kinds of upheaval in life that we realize there is a very real sense in which life lives us in addition to our living it. This is an unnerving thought, and many people who experience being overwhelmed by the power of strong emotions—disturbing thoughts and images and dreams so intense they stay throughout the day—are anxious to return to what they view as ordinary life. Others are permanently changed, and want to find ways to maintain contact with the powerful forces of soul and psyche. Living as if conscious life is all there is and living in relation to the activities of the unconscious are two quite different ways of life.

As for those of us who have mercifully been spared overwhelming tragedy, there are other opportunities to discover our own depths. Falling in love often presents us with the opportunity of experiencing a deeper reality. Feeling that someone was fated to come into one's life, having a sense that someone is a soul mate, appeals to a level of reality not referred to by our ongoing concerns with practical matters. It suggests that there is some meaning in life that is not created by us, but is there to be found. Falling in love also gives many people a sense that such powerful feelings have trans-human origins, that somehow the divine is connected with the love they feel.

Both grief and falling in love are to a great extent externally determined. No loss, no grief. No love-object, no love. These events can be uniquely powerful in forcing us into awareness of our inner lives. But they are not uniquely efficacious. There are gentler introductions to inner life. These gentler introductions involve attending to our inner experiences and finding a way to come into relation with them.

Connecting Creation and Discovery, the Voluntary and the Involuntary

One of the profoundest feelings of discovery in psychic life is connected with our discovery of those unconscious processes that are responsible for involuntary experience. We find ourselves saying things we didn't know we knew, yet immediately we recognize them as authentic for us. We discover, through seemingly random, autonomously appearing thoughts and associations features of ourselves we didn't know were there. We have strange dreams which nevertheless seem deeply meaningful, and whose content we recognize as uniquely our own. The unconscious speaks, and we have a sense of having discovered something that in some sense we knew all along. These kinds of inner experiences are not experiences of collecting new information. They are more like uncovering something forgotten, but something that has always been there. At the same time, having discovered them, coming into relation with them involves the creative and the voluntary. We decide to think more about the thoughts that have come to us, to use our imaginations to create a richer relation to our dreams. We have that immense pleasure that comes from being able to exercise our capacities for creation and discovery, our ability for both voluntary and involuntary experience all at once. We need not feel cut off from our deeper selves by will, nor need we feel that we must create ourselves and our meanings from nothing. And all of this allows us to come into a new relation with the externally determined. We have discovered what complex beings we are, and we have also discovered that when something is presented to us, when we have an encounter with the involuntary either inside or out, we need not be altogether reactive. We can be conscious and make choices about our behavior. Through attention and reflection, we can integrate creation, discovery, the voluntary, and the involuntary.

Knowing Reality, Working on Dreams

In what we think of as the common-sense view of the world, knowing reality is not difficult. All we have to do is look around. In the philosophical view of the empiricists that underlies our familiar scientific worldview, looking around becomes more complex, since we must connect our experiences to the external world, with which they are not identical. The problem of skepticism is insoluble; that is, we can never know with certainty that the world is identical to our experiences, we can never know with certainty exactly what the world is like apart from our experiences since we have only our experiences. Nevertheless, as Locke pointed out, we can know enough to get along. Reality in this sense is external, and something we come into relation with. It is implicitly contrasted with appearance, that is, how things appear to us, and the more closely we can connect our experiences of appearances to the external world, the better our contact with reality.

Experienced human reality is a complicated business. We do, of course, have daily, ongoing experiences of having a relation to the world. Some are successful in the sense that what we think is there really is there, and some are not. We can accurately count the number of chairs in a room, but mistake a Pekinese for a coyote on a walk in the park. However, the most important reality for most of us has to do with our relations to others. This is emotional reality, and how good we are at relating to this kind of reality determines to a surprising extent the quality of our lives. The notion of "relating" to this kind of reality is slightly misleading, since our own responses form a substantial part of it. To understand how this is so, the notion of projection is useful. Projection involves the attribution of qualities, motives, and attitudes to others whose origin is our own emotional structures—in Jungian terms, complexes. Other people remind us of the cast of characters of our childhoods and trigger emotional responses from the complexes formed by that childhood. This involves not only our unconscious attitudes to people who are perhaps long gone, but also the longings connected with unfulfilled needs, underdeveloped parts of ourselves, and even our relation to the divine. This rather mechanical-sounding process is not conscious and chosen, but often deeply unconscious. It structures our experience of the world both cognitively and emotionally. That is, we have beliefs about other people, and those beliefs are saturated with feeling. Anyone who has met someone unknown to her or him and taken a violent and often embarrassing dislike to her or him has experienced an acute version of this. All versions are not this obvious; our everyday thoughts and attitudes towards others are highly conditioned by our complexes and, since we live inside this reality, we may not notice until it becomes a problem. The ways in which it can become a problem are all too familiar: the person who leaves job after job because her or his co-workers seem to be so hard to get along with, the person who cannot sustain relationships because others don't seem to understand her or him, and a myriad of other difficulties that are part of the grit of everyday life.

The fact that this is called projection suggests that there might be another reality upon which this internally determined reality is projected. Suppose this is so. Is there some reason to believe that it is desirable to know what it is? Two reasons present themselves.

First, our relationships with other people prosper when other people feel "seen"; that is, when others feel that we are actually interested in them, can see things from their point of view and value them in themselves. It is not emotionally satisfying or even very interesting to be with people who are acting from a purely internally determined scenario. In such scenarios, other people are just placeholders, occasions for enacting the recurring and limited drama conditioned by complexes.

Second, in addition to the more familiar pleasures of relationship, there is an intrinsic pleasure in being able to be in contact with the reality of others. It relieves us of what is often experienced as the burden of self. This burden causes our experience to be limited, limiting, and repetitious. There is a deep emotional pleasure in being able to see others, to let some fresh energy into our psyches from without as well as from within. The novels of Iris Murdoch are full of accounts of people who are struggling with this difficulty, who are ruthless and insensitive as a result of self-absorption, and who are liberated when something, often tragedy, breaks through and forces them to pay attention to others.[8]

If it is desirable to contact that reality, how can we go about doing it? Though this suggests going about it completely backwards, the most effective way to begin to know the reality of others is to better understand the reality of ourselves. We need to become conscious of those projections so that we can come into a different relation with our complexes. This is a long, difficult process, but it can result in healing, compassion, and clarity of vision. It is this interior reality to which dreams offer access, perhaps unparalleled access. Emotional response and free association, to mention two conscious processes with roots in the unconscious, can also tell us a great deal about the activities of the unconscious, but dreams offer particularly rich and precise information. Furthermore, attention to dreams strengthens our connection with the unconscious, so that we experience ourselves differently. One of the things that makes projection so easy is the extent to which the conscious mind is split off from the unconscious. Jung discusses this throughout his works, but with particular emphasis in "The Transcendent Function."[9] In order to pay sustained attention to the complex and high-maintenance business of modern living, we need to be able to separate ourselves from conscious awareness of other processes taking place in the larger psyche. Attention to dreams means, among other things, that we are turning towards the larger psyche. Through attention to dreams, we can have more conscious access to our own reality, those feelings, images, thoughts, longings, and attitudes that constitute our own worldviews. And with that conscious knowledge, we are much better able to take in the reality of others.

Attention to dreams gives us access to the larger psyche, and this has consequences beyond self-knowledge and increased understanding of others. Complexes can only remain contained if they are unconscious. When we become conscious of them we open the door not only to knowledge of particular complexes, but also to contact with the deeper psyche. Possession by unconscious complexes is inherently confusing, since it involves a mingling of past and present, of emotion which has to do with things that have already happened and not what's happening now, with the frozen horror of trauma and the despair of being trapped in incomprehensible feelings. Emotionally, we cannot make even the most fundamental discrimination between our own feelings and those of others: the world is created by these interior conditions. When we begin to be able to identify complexes, we can also begin to experience our discrete existence, the differences between how we feel and how others see things, and this enables us, paradoxically, to move towards the depths of the psyche where the personal unconscious ends and the objective or collective unconscious begins. It creates the conditions for the breaking through of archetypal energies, the energies of the divine, because the strengthened ego is able to tolerate this breakthrough without being overwhelmed. And this gives us access to yet another level of reality.

The works of the mystics tell us that the divine is not somewhere else, but here and now. The Christian mystics experienced the presence of God in their own lives. In his book *The Psychoanalytic Mystic*, Michael Eigen connects the mysticism of religious experience with Bion's notion of O and Lacan's jouissance.[10] The experience of the Other, however it may be named, is a constant and enlivening possibility. Various contemplative and meditative practices increase our availability for this experience, because they can help us contact a deeper reality in the psyche. However, many people have great difficulty with these practices for reasons connected with unconscious complexes. Contemplative practice forces us into the presence of these complexes, which may be so fearful to some that contemplation is impossible. Another anxiety is the fragmentation of the ego. People who have powerful unconscious complexes do not have strong egos, they have rigid egos. A strong ego is flexible and permeable to incursions of unconscious experience. A rigid ego fears that any change could shatter it. In addition, people who have a great deal of unconfronted unconscious material often use what they think of as "spiritual life," which for them consists of a great deal of imagination and fantasy rather the discipline of daily practice, as an avoidance of the painful possibilities of consciousness. Work with dreams can be a gentle, relatively unthreatening way of approaching this unconscious material. Dreams are multileveled, so the dreamer can work at whatever level is most accessible, while keeping in mind that there is more should he or she choose to explore it. Work with dreams also helps us cultivate appropriate awe. The fact that the psyche has a rich, deep, and ultimately transcendent life of its own is truly awe inspiring. Our own individual psyches provide us with the possibility of a personal connection with the divine, whatever religious tradition we may or may not embrace. Without this kind of awe, we are deprived of a substantial aspect of our relation to the Otherness in life, which ranges from our own archetypally structured psyches to the ultimate experience of otherness, mystical union.

The process of coming into relation to reality is, like everything else in human life, a process of creation and discovery and an experience of both the voluntary and involuntary. In order to do the work that brings us into a better relation with reality, we need to understand and engage with who we are. Work on dreams is particularly well suited to both creating and discovering ourselves, to developing a relation to the involuntary activities of the unconscious. Dreams are a familiar phenomenon, usually thought of as ordinary life events. Often they receive little if any attention unless they are particularly charming, humorous, frightening, or awe inspiring. We have been dreaming as long as we can remember, so the arrival of a dream is not unexpected in the way that sudden intense emotion or a vision might be, nor as threatening as the more dramatic external events can be. Dreams come and go, and our relationship to them is often one of passing and temporary interest. Thus work with dreams is work with the familiar, and like any new relation to the familiar, it can be transformative. Work with dreams gives us the opportunity to see ourselves in a new way. It can enhance the realization of possibility of psychic depth, and it can do so in a relatively nonthreatening way, since work with dreams can be done in a number of ways and at a number of levels. Dream work tends to be self-reinforcing, since the pleasure in coming to know ourselves better can rival the pain that can be created by increased self-knowledge. Work on dreams can alter our sense of what it is to know ourselves. It can result in a heightened sense of our own complexity, a deepened experience of emotion, and often, surprisingly, in spiritual awakening.

The area of spiritual awakening is a particularly interesting one in work with dreams because it is often the most unexpected. People with some degree of psychological sophistication are not surprised to discover that they have hidden emotional lives. They may be surprised by just what the hidden emotions are, but not that they are there. It is not uncommon to have the sense that we have feelings that are not yet fully known. It makes sense to say, "I'm not sure how I feel about that," with the implication that there is feeling there, but we have not yet become fully conscious of what it is. Dreams can offer access to these deeper areas of feeling. As well, most of us are comfortable with the notion that there are thoughts to which we have a similar relation. Whatever one's analysis of unconscious thoughts, sometimes forming an opinion has as much to do with discovery as it does with rational process. When I was writing my doctoral thesis, I would often stop and attend carefully to thoughts that seemed to emerge out of the depths already formed. Most people who have written anything of any length are familiar with this kind of self-interrogation and the interesting results it brings. Theories are often created by a kind of dialogue between our rational, conscious points of view and those thoughts that seem to have been formed at a deeper level. Here too dreams can be helpful. When I was a graduate student at the University of Iowa, a friend who was a graduate student in mathematics told me the story of a fellow student of hers who was having great difficulty with his thesis. He needed to create an original theorem, but nothing was emerging. One night, in a dream, a theorem came to him. He awoke, and it still made sense. He wrote it down, constructed a proof, and before long was defending his thesis. One of his examiners commented on the originality of his theorem, and asked how he arrived at it. The student replied, "It came to me in a dream." Everyone laughed, assuming he was being cagey.

In the process of psychotherapy, dreams can offer us access to deeper aspects of our personal lives: painful memories and events, and many experiences and possibilities that have been put away and forgotten because they were too painful, frightening, and/or threatening to stay in consciousness.

That this is so has become an ordinary though not uncontroversial belief. Dreams about the divine, however, have a different status.

Though spiritual and religious dreams have been reported in every major religious tradition throughout human history, those of us living in contemporary Western culture do not find this an ordinary notion. We live in a complex, technology-dominated culture which values the satisfaction of material desire, often short-term desire, above virtually anything else. Established religion appears to have a different role in people's lives: a commitment no longer assumed, but still valued by some. Outside established religion, attitudes towards spiritual life vary considerably. Some of the most common are complete denial of its value, highly individualized notions of spiritual life, and a combination of longing and confusion. Thus when we have dreams that seem to be about something other than our personal issues, it can be disconcerting, confusing, and even frightening. We often don't know how to incorporate them into our lives. Even those who participate in established religious traditions (and here I have Christianity particularly in mind) can see dreams about the divine as unorthodox and even dangerous. Nevertheless, these dreams do occur.[11] In this book, I will examine a number of these dreams, and focus on how they have been understood by the people who had them. I will discuss these dreams from both Jungian and other spiritual perspectives, with a particular emphasis on the Jungian understanding of spiritual experience, that is, the assumption that spiritual experience is real because people have it, but that it may or may not have reference to something that exists outside the psyche. This is consistent with several different points of view. For example, the psychoanalyst Ana Maria Rizzuto, in *The Birth of the Living God*, argues that religious beliefs and experience are part of the transitional space described by Winnicott.[12] From a Jungian standpoint, these experiences are connected to the archetypal foundations of psychic life. From a spiritual (in the sense of a belief in the reality of a spiritual realm) standpoint, these dreams are a way of being in contact with the divine, which exists independently of our experience; though the divine exists independently of us, we experience its reality psychically.

Jung has a complex notion of our relation to the divine. It is basically experiential, but it is experiential with an underlying metaphysical view. Jung believes that the psyche is constituted by complexes whose cores are archetypal. Complexes are both archetypal and specific to individuals. Various manifestations of the archetypes have common themes, but each of us has a particular version of these themes. One of the major sources of the experience of meaning is emotional response and connection, and the emotions that form these responses and connections come from the complexes of the individual. These complexes are comprised of both cultural and individual archetypal material. The way we experience our lives, the meanings that events have for us and that fact that we are drawn to particular patterns of living are due the presence of archetypes. The archetypal structures form the subject matter of human life. For example, we are all children of parents, many of us are parents of children, and the value of family life in some form is a widespread feature of human experience. Thus we live out the archetypes of mother, father, child, family, and home. The experience of living in these patterns determines the contents of each individual complex. For example, if I am fortunate enough to have loving parents, my mother and father complexes will contain the images and feelings associated with these good experiences. I will internalize the good mother and the good father, my own experiences (images, feeling) gathered around an archetypal core. There are many archetypes, and human life is complex. These archetypes can be found in myth, art, and sacred text. They can also be found on television and in comic books. They are pervasive, because they are the ground of human life.

Not all archetypes have explicitly to do with the plot of life, though they must be lived out. The archetype of the shadow and the contrasexual archetypes (anima/animus) have to do with our abilities to be our whole selves. The shadow complex is formed through the rejection of parts of the personality the ego cannot tolerate because of the familial and cultural contexts in which the person finds her or himself. The contents of the shadow are usually thought of as qualities that are objectively negative: greed, selfishness, jealousy. However, there may be archetypal contents that, described differently, are positive. For example, in families and other environments, such as, for example, academic environments, where "cool" and knowingness are highly valued, spontaneity and simplicity may be sources of shame. They may be relegated to the shadow as foolishness and stupidity, but upon reconsideration may turn out to be highly valued. Work on the shadow can be particularly fruitful for the development of authenticity, since it is often the most individual aspects of the person that have to be rejected. By the same token, the contrasexual complex contains those aspects of the person that are unacceptable to the gender identity offered in a particular family and culture. These too may be some of the most individual aspects of the person. And both have particularly to do with the ego complex, which is our conscious conception of ourselves. Whatever does not fit in there must be relegated to the unconscious in some form, and the ego's limitations prevent some unconscious contents from emerging, thus prevent psychic development.

Perhaps the most important archetypal representation in the psyche is the archetype of the Self, the archetypal representation of the divine in the psyche. The Self both contains the psyche and is at its center. The Self is the source of a divine energy that is both transforming and terrifying. The Self is not the divine, but is connected to and represents the divine since we cannot experience the divine directly (though the exact nature of this relation is difficult to describe precisely).[13] Jung believed that spiritual life can be described as the ego's forming a relation to the Self such that the ego becomes relativized. That is, the ego does not disappear, but the illusion of control that is an aspect of the ego's attitude disappears. The ego defers to the purposes of the Self. To put this in spiritual terms, we defer to the will of God. Jungians describe this relation as the ego-Self axis. The Self is the ultimate source of psychic energy and it is the source of our sense of what kind of life is authentic for us. Through being connected to and knowing the Self (though of course we can never know the Self completely), we know ourselves at the deepest possible level.

Why it is important to attend to our experiences of human life as archetypally structured? Jung saw archetypal energies as "the organs of God."[14] What this meant to him was that apparently ordinary human life and experience has a divine core, and can be experienced at a much deeper level than we might have supposed. It also means that what happens in our lives is not just random, but is a part of an archetypal pattern that is unfolding in each of us. Each of us has a given identity, in the sense that our lives are determined by archetypal themes, and each of us has an individual version of this identity that it is part of our spiritual work to live out as fully as possible. This view resembles Aristotle's views about general human essence and individual versions of it. Thus our lives are a complex of creation and discovery, of the voluntary and the involuntary.

Jungian psychology has been a resource for many people's spiritual journeys. There are a number of reasons for this. First of all, there is the emotional impact of Jungian psychology itself. For people who have a strong need to live a highly individualized and autonomous life, Jungian psychology is moving and inspiring. Jung himself lived a highly individualized life in a society characterized by strong demands for conformity. He continued to be creative in his own life until the time of his death. His theories reflect his sense of the importance of individual life and offer a vision of the possibility of continuous creativity. Furthermore, he connects the development of individuality with developing a relation to the divine. For Jung, the development of individuality is accomplished through inner work. This is a process of self-knowledge, self-understanding, making what is unconscious conscious, and to the best of one's abilities, knowing and accepting the whole self. It is through making a connection with the Self, the archetypal representation of the divine in the psyche, that one may come into an individual relation with the divine. For Jung, the path to spiritual life is through the inner life. Jung believed that spiritual life is essentially experiential: spiritual life that supports psychic development must be based on our individual experiences of the spirit. These may come through dreams, visions, and creativity. There is no substitute for experience in spiritual life, particularly not belief in the dogmas of a religious tradition simply because this is what one has been taught. This kind of belief is experientially deadening because it requires us to stifle our individual responses to these dogmas and to life itself, and Jung saw these responses as, spiritually, the cutting edge. Emotional response is the manifestation of the archetypal core of the complexes that structure the psyche, and it is through emotional response as well as the experience of imagery that we come to understand the unique manifestations of archetypal life in each of us. As I mentioned above, Jung believed the archetypes are the "organs of God." Because of the dynamic qualities of the archetypes, I prefer to think of them as the energies of God, at work structuring the psyche and providing each of us with the potential to make an authentic connection with the divine.

These views of Jung's have had great emotional impact on many people who feel spiritually stifled and blocked. Archetypally, Jung is often experienced as a kind of spiritual father and the emotional effect of his writing has often provided a way into spiritual life through making people emotionally receptive to spiritual life as he describes it. It is his overall image of spiritual life as the deepest expression of the individual that provides this impact. This is in addition to the actual details of the theories themselves, which, to an emotionally receptive mind can offer the kind of profound understanding that is the most satisfying form of intellectual activity.

Does this mean that Jungian psychology is itself a kind of spiritual path? Yes and no, depending on what one includes in the concept of the spiritual path. Those Jungians who are particularly concerned with spiritual life[15] emphasize spiritual life as contact with the energies of the Self in the psyche, the ego-Self axis. If the ego-Self axis is strong, our relation with the Self will be vital and ongoing. We will experience imagery, synchronicities, dreams, and transpersonal emotions that enrich our everyday lives. We will experience our lives as meaningful because we will feel a strong connection to the divine in the psyche in such a way that we can see that the purposes of the divine are being served by difficulty and suffering and that our own increase of consciousness is an incarnation of the divine. This is clearly a rich spiritual life of a highly individualized kind. However, traditionally spiritual life has existed not just through the individual's experience of the spirit, but also in the context of a relation with a larger tradition which provides other kinds of archetypally based experiences, such as ritual and teaching. Jung himself believed that one of the most successful forms of spiritual life was the ability to return to the spiritual tradition that provided one's spiritual formation and understand it in a new way. From the standpoint of emotional satisfaction, this seems to me to be true. In addition, there is the question of the container for spiritual growth.

Jung's last work was in the area of alchemy. He believed that the alchemical process is an objective correlative of the transformation and growth of the psyche. Crucial to the alchemical process is the concept of the container in which the alchemical transformations take place. In the psyche, the container is provided by the Self, which contains the whole psyche. In the analytic process, the relationship between the therapist and client is the container for the transformation of both therapist and client, though the emphasis is of course on the transformation of the client. The analytic container allows the energies of the Self to be invoked for both client and therapist. The image of the container suggests that the energies of transformation need to be "held" while something new is taking shape, and that the presence of the container is essential to the process. The same is true of the specifically spiritual journey. While for a Jungian all inner work is spiritual since the complexes have an archetypal core, it is also true that some inner work is highly concentrated on the relation to the personal unconscious and strengthening the ego, while other work is highly concentrated on the ego-Self axis. It is this latter that constitutes the specifically spiritual journey. Which containers are particularly appropriate to the spiritual journey? One candidate is the relation between the spiritual director and directee. This provides the same kind of container that is created by the therapist and client. Another candidate is a religious tradition/institution such as a church. I will discuss this at greater length toward the end of this book. For the moment, I want to briefly put forward a modest proposal. Though I recognize the many failings and shortcomings of organized religion, failings and shortcomings that are shared by every institution connected to a tradition that constitutes society, nevertheless I believe there is something to be said for participation in a religious tradition. The liturgy enables us to experience an outward manifestation of an inward condition. We have the advantage of the experiences and insights of those who have gone before us. The church as container can connect us to the energies of the Self. There is another way in which the church can be a container, and it is this I particularly want to discuss later at greater length. If the church is part of the tradition that provided us with spiritual formation, it can become carrier of the archetypal energies of home. This is possible even if the church of one's choice is not the particular part of the tradition that provided spiritual formation, but it is an even stronger possibility if it is.

Now, however, let us consider what constitutes dreaming about the divine.

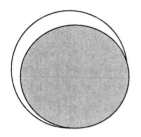

3

Dreaming about the Divine

How can we identify dreams about the divine? There are two main criteria. The first is affective quality. Some dreams about the divine have a numinous quality that carries with it a sense of self-evident transcendence and meaning. The quality of the experience itself produces in the dreamer a sense of having encountered something of a different metaphysical kind, not only from ordinary human experience, but from most dream experience. Such dreams are often life changing and result in an increased faith in a higher or deeper power. However, numinosity is not always a peaceful and inspiring experience. Some dreams contain emotions of enormous power that seem to indicate heightened significance. Lionel Corbett argues that powerful emotion is an indication of the presence of archetypal energy: "The numinosum announces its presence by its affective intensity. . . . The direct experience of spirit, or archetype, is always accompanied by such affect, for instance as part of a complex, or simply in the form of interest or emotional investment. . . . In practice this means that the presence of intense affect always indicates the presence of the archetype."[1]

Thus while some numinous dreams bring with them an increased sense of peace and meaning, others can be frightening and overwhelming, or involve intense feelings that are difficult to categorize. As an example of this, Jung writes about the experiences of Nicholas of Flue, also known as Bruder Klaus. Bruder Klaus is reported to have had experiences of the divine so intense and terrifying that the expression on his face was permanently changed, frightening others. Over the years, Bruder Klaus developed interpretations of these experiences that were consistent with

Christian doctrine, but these were reinterpretations. His initial experiences seemed to defy understanding, going beyond any categories he had and not consistent with church teachings of a loving God that was at least to some degree comprehensible.[2]

However, affective intensity is not the only criterion. Subject matter plays an important role, especially in the dreams of people who are in the process of spiritual formation and/or re-formation, and are searching for a highly individualized version of the divine. Dreams will often contain images such as angels or altars that refer to the dreamer's previous religious or spiritual experience, or that are associated with some new possibility of experience of the divine, such as religious imagery from traditions other than the dreamer's. These images may not have a strong numinous quality. It is not uncommon for people to be frightened by the prospect of numinous experience even as they long for it, and the imagery will sometimes appear without the powerful affect as a kind of gentle approach by the divine.

A Basic Framework

The relationship to the divine can permeate every aspect of our lives, so it is not surprising that not all dreams about the divine are focused on the supremacy of the Self. Many of these dreams represent the way the divine is most active in our lives at the moment, which could be anywhere and in any way. From a Jungian perspective, all dreams are about the divine because all dreams have archetypal content. However, some dreams are more conspicuously about the divine than others in the sense that the presence of the divine in some form is either, through affective intensity and/or subject matter, the focus of the dream or that focusing on the presence of the divine in interpretation provides the deepest sense of meaning in the dream for the dreamer. Working with dreams at this level can be challenging and require a deep level of spiritual attunement on the part of the therapist, analyst, or spiritual director. To understand why, it will be helpful to set up a basic framework for talking about various kinds of inner work and the corresponding kinds of work with dreams. There are three fundamental methods of doing inner work: therapy as counseling, psychodynamic psychotherapy and analysis, and spiritual direction. Let us examine each one.

Therapy as counseling covers a wide ground. There are many kinds of psychotherapies that address themselves to various issues in people's lives: family-of-origin issues, abuse issues, mid-life issues, and so on. If I had to characterize the purpose of counseling, I would say that it works to help people become themselves more deeply and confidently. This entails finding healing for childhood wounds, ways of getting "unstuck" from paralyzing life situations, improving communication and relationship skills, and increasing our generative capacities for the sake of our children and loved ones. In general, these increased capacities mean a strengthening of ego in the positive sense, a pleasurably increased sense of self and confidence, and a more resilient response to life's vicissitudes. This in turn allows us to integrate repressed material, to feel freer in ourselves, less driven by unconscious forces. When we work with dreams in this kind of therapy, we are mostly focused on how the dream images are connected with our damaged, unknown, and/or undeveloped selves, and how this affects our functioning in the world. These dreams can be experienced as having great depth and meaning, especially for people who have had to repress a great deal of emotion and personhood in order to survive shattering childhoods.

Psychodynamic psychotherapy and analysis share with therapy as counseling the ability to help us live more fully and deeply. In the best instances, this kind of therapeutic and analytic work can lead to profound personal transformation and healing. There is an emphasis on self-knowledge: even when we cannot easily change ourselves, our experience of life is altered by bringing what has been unconscious into consciousness. In Jungian terms, to be able to be conscious of our complexes, of their power in our lives, the patterns of feeling and behavior they generate, is to have an increased sense of self and to reduce our own sense of victimization by our own thoughts and feelings. In addition, analysis offers us a way to understand and participate in the deep dynamics of the psyche. This can happen through the transforming relationship between analyst and analysand, the artwork and journaling that accompany analysis, and through direct experience in dreams. Most people in analysis have the experience of having at least one and often more numinous dreams, in which the images of the dream have an unusual and compelling power. In these dreams, we feel we have been in the presence of something beyond the human and the personal. In Jungian terms, such dreams are often the way the transcendent function and the archetypal energies from the collective unconscious make themselves felt. These dreams can be related to spiritual life, in the sense that they can be the occasion of transformation and an indication of what, symbolically, is especially meaningful to us. The work of analysis provides a context for spiritual search and deeper contact with spiritual resources, and the dreams that occur in analysis often reflect this.

Spiritual direction is different from both psychodynamic psychotherapy and analysis and therapy as counseling. It focuses on a relationship to the divine and disidentification with the ego. In the Christian tradition, spiritual direction has been a practice reserved for clergy and those who live in religious communities. From the time of the Desert Fathers, those who have committed themselves to spiritual life have sought help with becoming more open to the divine and with discernment in relation to the intense experiences that arise in deep prayer and contemplative life. This has been called discernment of spirits: which experiences come from God, which from Satan. We would describe this differently now, but discernment continues to be an important focus of spiritual direction. Often contemporary spiritual direction is informed by Jungian and psychodynamic theories, so that issues of discernment are described in terms of what comes from unconscious complexes or unresolved developmental issues and what comes from the deeper self; in the case of Jungian theory, discernment seeks to identify what comes from the Self. Other traditional issues in spiritual direction have been developing a rule of life, understanding the relevance of scripture to one's own life, and bringing more spirituality into relationships. Traditionally, spiritual direction does not take place as often as therapy, the director and directee meeting perhaps once a month, perhaps less often. In contemporary spiritual direction, director and directee may meet more often.

More recently, the practice of spiritual direction has become of interest to many who are neither clergy nor lifelong members of religious communities. We live in a time in which there are significant numbers of people disaffected from the religious traditions in which they were brought up, yet have great spiritual longing. Spiritual direction has been a way of entering into spiritual life without necessarily committing to a religious organization. At the same time, spiritual direction itself is in the process of change. Spiritual directors have begun to incorporate the insights of psychoanalysis and other psychological theories, so that they can work with the deep personal issues, such as abuse and dysfunctional relationships, that often arise in the context of spiritual direction. These issues are not the focus of spiritual direction, but they can be included in spiritual direction and seen as a part of one's spiritual journey. Work with dreams in spiritual direction will incorporate features of dream work in therapy and analysis, but it will have an additional feature: attention to and focus on the divine, with the accompanying lack of emphasis on ego development. This does not mean that ego development does not take place in spiritual direction. Paradoxically, the deeper the contact with the divine, the stronger the ego becomes. The ego does not become dominant or rigid, but rather strong and flexible, open to new experience. Ann Ulanov describes the ego's activity in connection with the Self: "Our ego is toughened and loosened from its moorings to do this housing of the Self. Feeling certain and at ease in its capacity to receive, translate, and transmit the Self, the ego also sees that its own workings are manifestations of the Self, not ultimate in themselves. Even more loosening is the perception that the Self which feels like this big center is neither spirit nor God per se but that within us which knows about God or the spirit. It is this knowing unknowing that gives us the sense, I believe, of that center living in us which is not us, so near to St. Paul's description of it, 'Not I, but Christ lives in me.'"[3]

What does this mean in practice? In a moment, I will offer some illustrative case material, but first I want to say a few general things. People come into spiritual direction with the intention of deepening their relationship with the divine. Sometimes they have very clear ideas about the nature of the divine and sometimes not.

Though this is an oversimplification, for the sake of this discussion I would like to divide those who seek spiritual direction into two categories. The first is the most familiar; people who already have spiritual commitments and want to expand and deepen them, giving them a more personal meaning. I have in my practice a number of lifelong Anglicans, committed churchgoers, who, at a certain point, realized that spiritual life could be more deeply experienced. For these people, spiritual direction can offer ways to explore the faith they already have and, through contemplation and dream work, they can have experiences of the divine more powerful and personal than those that occur in the context of corporate worship. These people are often extremely receptive to dream work (unless there is some theological reason for distrusting dreams) and, for those who already have some kind of contemplative practice, take to it very easily. When I first gave dream groups at Christ Church Cathedral in Vancouver, I was struck by the receptivity I found. Many of the people in these groups were not particularly psychologically minded, but they were spiritually minded, often having a daily spiritual practice. They entered into dream work with trust and ease, because their own inner lives were already vividly real to them as a result of ongoing spiritual practice. For those who are already committed to a spiritual tradition, dream work can be an adventure, a way of incorporating into their spiritual lives feelings and images that are different from those familiar ones from scripture, liturgy, and so on. Drawing on Jung's views about the collective unconscious, it is an opportunity to experience symbolic imagery from other sources as meaningful. For this reason, these people often experience dream work as surprising. Expecting to find representations of spiritual life in their dreams that reflect their conscious religious commitments, they often discover symbolism that is entirely new to them, and new ways of understanding symbolism that is already familiar. As well, they often experience the relation of dream work to their conscious religious experience as a version of personal interpretation of scripture and liturgical language. That is, they are able to bring deeply personal meaning to images and language that is familiar and unexamined. For example, they can connect their own personal spiritual journeys with the life of Christ and their most cherished biblical texts. Dreams can provide a surprising, sometimes disturbing, stimulating, enriching addition to the spiritual lives they already have. Dream work can also increase their sense of lived spirituality. By being able to connect dreams with everyday life, people can experience a greater depth of meaning. This is especially important for people whose major spiritual activity has been corporate worship and church work. It is often a revelation to discover images of the divine in the world, in their lives, and in the activities that fill their days. There can be a deeper sense of connection with God's plan for them, especially if they develop a sense of the divine within. In Jungian terms, dreams are driven by the Self. In spiritual terms, the divine sends the dreams. In Christian terms, we might say that dreams can be part of our ongoing relation with the Holy Spirit.

The second category of person I have found in spiritual direction I would call seekers. These are people who have a profound longing for spiritual life, but who are not involved in any religious community or tradition. Perhaps they had a religious upbringing from which they have drifted away, don't find meaningful, or reject, or have had bad experiences with organized religion. Many of these people in my practice are artists, creative people who have spiritual experiences that do not fit easily into a religious framework as they understand it. This longing is not some sort of simple wish, but can involve real suffering, a profound wish for meaning that doesn't seem to come, an awareness of another level that they are not able to experience. They may believe, theoretically, in some sort of higher power or divine force but be unable to get any farther than that. They want a deeper connection with the divine, but don't know how to find it. For these people, dream work is a way into spiritual life which, from their point of view, is uncontaminated with specific religious prejudices. Initially, they often seek a nonsectarian spiritual life. That is, they seek a personal relationship with the divine from the inside out, through the symbols offered in their dreams.

Interestingly, the dreams of those committed to a particular religious tradition are often not that different, either in content or interpretation, from the dreams of seekers. The biggest difference is the presence of a larger set of beliefs in religiously committed people and the connecting of dreams to those beliefs in order to make them meaningful. Seekers do not have this larger belief system, and it is the absence of this system that is often the source of the dissatisfaction and suffering that brings them to spiritual direction. What they are actually seeking is not so much spiritual direction, which is usually done from the standpoint of a particular tradition, as spiritual formation, the discovery and development of a spiritual path. For these people, dream work can have immense significance, because dreams are one of their only connections with the world of the spirit. Dream work can be used as a tool to build a kind of private spiritual life, perhaps even leading to a spiritual practice. This can be a profound and satisfying experience, though it has its limitations. If this is as far as it goes, it can lead to experiencing spiritual life as essentially private, which most people in the end find unsatisfactory. Some connection with a larger body seems to be an intrinsic part of spiritual longing. I have often thought that the fact that the offices of the Cathedral Centre for Spiritual Direction were in a church was experienced as an attraction even for the people who said they had no interest in organized religion. Being in a church offered a way for otherwise unconnected people to connect with a larger spiritual world with a long history without feeling too threatened. In my experience, it seems very likely that, in order to have a serious spiritual life, we must develop a relationship with a religious tradition with whose wisdom and history we can be in dialogue. Personal experience is not adequate to introduce us to the widest possibilities of spiritual life. Spiritual life is private in the sense that we experience it from the inside, but this is not enough. We also need to feel contained from the outside, to be connected with a larger spiritual context, a history of spiritual experience we can draw on, and some kind of corporate worship. This enhances our sense of the divine and the spirit as going beyond our individual egos and helps live out the relativization of the ego in forms other than contemplation. To be part of a larger religious tradition also fosters humility in the face of the religious lives and experiences of others and of a variety of manifestations of the divine that are different from one's own. Humility is a crucial aspect of both emotional and spiritual life.

Dreams

Dreams play an important part in my work with both clients and spiritual directees. In general, when people start working with me, I ask them to record their dreams. The dreams in this book are nearly all literal transcriptions of dreams from the dream journals of clients and directees. Where this is not the case, they are the dreams of the clients or directees as I have recorded them, but this is very unusual.

I want now to talk about the actual interpretation of dreams. I have listed three types of inner work: therapy as counseling, psychodynamic therapy/analysis, and spiritual direction. These correspond to three different ways of looking at dreams. It is my sense that nearly all dreams can be interpreted in each of the three ways, and all contain several elements.

First of all, dreams can be existential—that is, they can be about our relationship to the world, our world. The characters in the dream may actually be our husbands, wives, partners, children, and so on, and the dream may be about our unconscious ways of being in and seeing these relationships and their significance on our lives. They may contain valuable information about our life in the world, things we need to notice but have not noticed, aspects of reality that are essential to being in relation to reality and living with integrity.

Second, dreams can be about our inner worlds. Every part of the dream is a part of myself, and the interaction among the elements of the dream is an image of the interaction of these elements. This is an important way of interpreting dreams in analysis and psychodynamic work, and it is often experienced as deeper than existential work. It offers one of the most important and satisfying experiences inner work can offer; the confirmation and validation of subjectivity in depth. Many people fully experience themselves as real for the first time when they begin to understand their own inner complexity through work on their dreams. It gives them a sense of their own depth, of the partial quality of consciousness in relation to the unconscious, and of the importance of contact with unconscious. This sense of the existence of an inner world that is autonomous, not controllable by will and ego, is the beginning of inner life as spiritual life. In fact, many people experience this kind of dream work as so meaningful and moving that they can come to feel that this new relation to subjectivity is spiritual life. It is my guess that people who seem to sacralize Jungian psychology are having this new and profound experience of inner depths.

Third, dreams can be about our relation with the divine. This is perhaps the most difficult kind of interpretation but it is also the deepest. Some of these dreams are intense experiences of numinous imagery that resist any sort of analysis. There is nothing more to be said about these dreams, though it can be satisfying to represent them in artwork, both because it is intrinsically satisfying to express them and because they are important symbols to have in our lives. These dreams are perhaps the most familiar versions of dreams having to do with the divine. However, there are many other kinds of dreams that express aspects of the divine. As in the case of Bruder Klaus, there are varieties of affective intensity that are more experience than image. In his book *The Psychoanalytic Mystic*, Michael Eigen discusses Bion's notion of O and Lacan's notion of jouissance, both experiences rather than images, and both the experience of some sort of ultimate otherness which is also life giving.[4] From a Jungian perspective, dreams can express important archetypal themes, such as the mystical marriage, being guided by wisdom figures, or the birth of the divine in the soul. There are dreams that express the difficulty of spiritual life and the relationship to the divine, dark dreams that may or may not feel numinous, but can be terrifying.[5] There are dreams that have fleeting images of the divine, such as angels, that may occur in the midst of existential concerns or inner work. These can often be a kind of preview of experiences to come.

One of the most important aspects of doing dream work with clients is developing a sense about which of these levels to begin with, since the same dream can have different meanings depending on the level selected. The deepest work is done through understanding how the dream works at each of these levels. If a client can come to see how the same themes resonate in everyday life, psychic life, and relationship with the divine, she or he can come as close as a human being can to seeing her or himself as a whole, in all of her or his complexity.

The following example illustrates how dreams work at each of these levels, and why it is so important to address each one. It belongs to a former client in spiritual direction. Jim is a man in his fifties who, at the time of having this dream, had gone through an intensely difficult time in his life. This was a vivid and painful dream.

A Dream of Humiliation

I am in prison and I am in torn and ragged clothes. I am in a brightly lit, bare room and am forced by the guards to strip and I do, feeling more and more humiliated.

At the existential level, this dream had strong meaning for Jim. He had been through a wrenching and adversarial divorce that left him financially strapped. He had just experienced a series of business difficulties that had resulted in his being unable to get work in his field. He had been wrongly accused of fraud, unsupported by his professional association, and left without any sense of what to do next. In addition, his second wife, who has a chronic illness, had begun to suffer debilitating symptoms after a long period of remission. His relations with his family of origin had become strained. He felt thoroughly stripped and humiliated.

This dream was also meaningful to him at the inner level. His parents had been both proud and envious of him. Both were controlling and tended to take credit for his accomplishments. Both used humiliation as a way to control him. Furthermore, his mother was critical of and disappointed in him because of his divorce, of which she disapproved. She made it clear to him that she felt he had disgraced his family. He felt this humiliation deeply and had internalized his mother's value system; he hurt and humiliated himself, continuing to judge himself by her standards, and thus kept himself in jail. Finally, these internalized parents continually berated him for his career difficulties, for which, though there was plenty of evidence to the contrary, he continued to blame himself.

However, the most deeply felt significance for him occurred in the area of his relation to the divine. He is a lifelong, devout Christian, and this dream occurred on Good Friday. For him, the dream showed that he was walking Christ's path, being stripped for humiliation and crucifixion, with its implications of resurrection to come. This sense of meaning in his suffering gave him hope, and expectation of the possibility of expanded life, which did indeed happen for him. He ended by finding more meaningful work, work that he had originally wanted to do but had been persuaded to forego by his ambitious mother, and a much deeper sense of connection to a loving God.

This dream could have been appropriately interpreted on each of these three levels, and each was meaningful to him. But the deepest experienced meaning for him occurred when the third level was added. It made him view his whole experience of loss and humiliation in a different way, as part of his spiritual journey. This dream demonstrates vividly the sharp contrast between the point of view of the conscious self and the point of view of the divine. From the point of view of the conscious self, the experience of the dream is horrible. The setting is horrible, the feelings are horrible, what he is forced to do is horrible. In the dream, he is completely in the grip of this experience, and this reflected his actual life experience. However, when he reflected on the dream, he was able to see it from the standpoint of the Self/divine. From that standpoint, his suffering was a prelude to and necessary part of transformation. Many dark dreams have this paradoxical quality: they are bad dreams, even nightmares, from the point of view of the conscious self, but they put the suffering of the conscious self in a completely different context, which transforms the meaning of the dream. This is why this third level of meaning is so important. It becomes especially important if we think of the origin of dreams.

One of the most curious features of dream life is its apparent randomness. One might suppose that a really efficient unconscious would provide dreams by subject matter: dreams about mothers until we have worked these issues through, then dreams about fathers, and so on. However, dreams seem either not to be in any particular order, or to be in an order which is very difficult to discover. If we assume that the Self is the container of the psyche and in some sense orders psychic experience, then it seems to make sense to say that the Self ultimately determines the subject matter and order of dreams. If this is so, then presumably the Self has some purpose that may be discovered in the dream. Thus if we do not penetrate to the third level of meaning, we will have missed perhaps the ultimate purpose of the dream, the Self's manifestation. In this case, Jim would have seen his dream as a summing up of his suffering rather than as living out his version of the Christian myth.

Let us examine another example, one that involves not suffering but pleasure, and which was also experienced by the client as meaningful at all three levels. Jeanette is a woman in her sixties who has struggled with a number of emotional and spiritual issues for some time. This is one of several dreams in which she experienced the presence of the divine.

In the Woodshed

I am in the woodshed. It is very vivid—I can smell the wood, and I like the woodshed and being in it very much. There is a window, and through it I can see a large snow owl perched on a fence post, like a sentry. Inside, I see several blond ferret-like creatures scamper out from under the wood pile, up the wall, and out of the woodshed. Then I notice that there are two baby snow owls perched high in the woodshed. The dream occurs in daytime, and it has a good feeling.

This is a dream that works at every level. At the existential level, Jeanette felt that the dream was about the end of a relationship that had been painful and difficult. She associated the ferrets with her feelings about her former partner's behavior: hiding, scurrying, and finally running away. She also associated the ferrets with feeling that her former partner was finally out of her life after a long period of ambivalence and grieving. The woodshed is a good place for her; she loved the woodshed as child, with the smell of newly cut wood, the feeling of coziness and containment. She also associates the woodshed with her father, whom she loved dearly; she enjoyed being in the woodshed with him when he was cutting wood. From an existential point of view, the dream seems to indicate that she is coming to a better place, perhaps a sense of her own life as determined more by her beloved and good-natured father rather than her controlling and guilt-wielding mother, it is a place where she feels good, and a place that is connected with a happy memory from an otherwise rather difficult childhood. She is very responsive to nature, and the presence of the owls seems to suggest a sense of being able to be connected with the natural world, part of a whole.

From the standpoint of inner work, the woodshed seems to offer an image of a happier, safer, container, an ego cleansed of disturbing forces (the ferrets). The window connecting with the outdoors suggests that this container is permeable rather than being cut off from unconscious forces. The presence of the owls inside and out suggests the possibility of knowledge, wisdom both present in consciousness and also present even more forcefully in the larger psyche that contains the ego.

From the spiritual standpoint, the snow owl seems to be an image of the divine. The owl carries the double aspect of both wisdom and death—in Greek mythology, the owl is associated with Athena and wisdom, while in many other mythologies, it is considered a bird of ill omen and death. In this sense it carries the associations of both wisdom and mortality. Jeanette saw the owl as a benevolent being, watching over her, and not a warning or a bad omen. Since she has been thinking about death, as is appropriate to her stage in life, the benevolent owl may be an indication that death is becoming less fearful to her, and she will find wisdom before it comes. The presence of the baby owls inside the woodshed seems to me to be another indication of the presence of the divine. Several pre-Socratic philosophers describe the presence of the divine in the human being as Pythagoras does: as a piece taken from the larger divine. In the Jewish tradition, human beings are often char-acterized as having a spark from the larger light of the divine. Both of these ways of characterizing our relation to the divine represent us as having a smaller bit of a larger divine being. Jeanette has baby owls in her woodshed, small "bits" of the larger being who sits watching over the world outside the woodshed. The luminous whiteness of the owl seems to emphasize its special-ness. Jeannette had a sense of the specialness and importance of the owl she could see through the window, and a good feeling about the baby owls, her own "bit" of the divine. The dream seems to characterize Jeanette's relation to the divine as being close and "homey"—owls in the woodshed, not angels in the church.

It is interesting to note that Jeanette is a lifelong and devout Catholic, but the images of the divine in her dreams are not Christian. I have worked with a large number of Christians in both my psychotherapy and spiritual direction practices, and their dreams are full of images of the natural world and from other mythologies, as well as Christian imagery. This imagery is just as mean-ingful to them as Christian imagery, and it seems likely that the presence of a great many images of the natural world is a kind of compensation for the limits of some traditional Christian attitudes towards nature. This does not apply only to Christianity. Any tradition to which we commit ourselves has limits, and the unconscious will work to supplement the conscious imagery that is so meaningful to us with other images of the divine to enrich our spir-itual lives. Any religious tradition has specific ways of envisioning God that by no means exhaust the possibilities, and, as James Hall points out in his book *The Unconscious Christian*, the religious function in the psyche will choose whatever imagery meets the requirements of the psyche.[6] To put it another way, the divine will appear in the form that is most meaningful to the dreamer not just at a conscious level, but at the level of the whole psyche.

These dreams each illustrate the importance of addressing all three levels of meaning. By understanding the dreams in terms of our personal and lived life, we bring the activities of the divine into our lives at the experiential level rather than seeing the divine as something that is exclusively transcendent and "above" us. What is also interesting about these dreams is the variety of sym-bolism, though the dreamers have similar conscious religious commitments: one is an Anglican, the other a Catholic. One dreams of himself walking Christ's path of suffering and humiliation as he deals with the difficulties of his life, the other experiences the divine as a natural force of great beauty and power, watching over her as she struggles with a relationship and the past. Both experienced these dreams as enhancing the meaning of their lived expe-rience, giving suffering significance, and giving both the sense that, though they struggled and suffered, God was not absent but participating. Lionel Corbett points out that the experience of the divine often enters our lives through the damaged parts of ourselves, because in these areas of the psyche, the border between conscious and unconscious is thinner.[7] In both of these instances, the dreamers experienced the divine in the context of challenging life situations, the kinds of situations described by Jaspers as boundary situations. Both experienced struggle, suffering and their own historicity in the sense of coming from particular families of origin. Both experienced guilt, loss, and disappointment, and both experienced increased energy, and a change in viewpoint and ways of being with the difficulties in their lives.

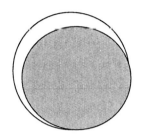

4

Dreams of Help, Comfort, and New Life

In the last chapter, we saw that dreams about the divine can give meaning to experiences in waking life, especially experiences of suffering. In both of the dreams cited, suffering has taken place and the dreamers are offered a different context for their suffering. There are other ways in which the presence of the divine can be called forth by suffering. These are dreams in which healing takes place, and in which a personal relation to the divine is experienced as part of that healing. By "healing" I mean both comfort and change for the better. These dreams are dreams of comfort, and offer the healing that can take place through divine comfort. Dreams of comfort present us with images of the divine that speak directly in a comforting way to our suffering. They represent perhaps the most accessible and nonthreatening way of being in contact with the divine. They often occur when the dreamer has been undergoing an extended period of suffering and is feeling not only the absence of human comfort, but also a sense of the absence of the divine. They often come to the desperate. When I was collecting dreams for this book, by far the greatest number of dreams I found fell into the categories of dreams of help, comfort, and the breaking through of new life. When we think of Jaspers's description of boundary situations, it seems uncontroversial to say that life is tough. It is tough just having to contend with the difficulties raised by the basic situations of life that are part of our historicity: suffering, guilt, death, struggle, disappointment, and loss are in themselves stressful, in addition to specific situations of pain and difficulty. There are enough of these situations in life that all the resources that the psyche can offer are called for, and one way these resources can be accessed is through dreams. In this straightforward way, we are offered nourishment by the divine: comfort and help when it is needed, renewal when our old lives are passing away. Not all of these dreams are unambiguously positive. Some of them contain sorrow, loss, and doubt as well as comfort, but all of them are predominantly comforting, helpful, and enlivening.

The following dream belongs to Heather, a client in spiritual direction who had undergone a long period of intense suffering, many times coming close to despair. Her family of origin was callous and critical, and her husband had recently committed suicide, leaving her with a small child. Her husband's suicide was completely unexpected, and she felt the only thing that had saved her from completely breaking down was the comfort of her church community. She had only recently joined the community and, for the first time in her life, she was surrounded by willing and compassionate support. But though this was helpful to her, she was still suffering terribly. Her husband's family blamed her for his suicide (though there was no realistic reason for them to do so), her child was devastated, and she was desperately lonely. The marriage had been an unhappy one, and she blamed herself (though again, there was no realistic reason for her to do so). Though surrounded by comfort on the outside, because of her cold and critical family she had no internalized sources of comfort and support. During this time, she had the following dream.

God as Comforter

> I dreamed that I was sad and alone, and God said to me, cover yourself with this coverlet and you will be comforted. The coverlet was like a brocade still life, covered in rich tapestry of fruit and flowers, very dark and rich, and it made me warm and comforted at once.

In one sense, the meaning of this dream is obvious. Heather needed comfort and comfort came from what she experienced as a transcendent source. But the meaning of the dream is deeper. One of the characteristics of Heather's family, her childhood relationship to God, and of her marriage was nonresponsiveness. In her family, she tried as hard as she could to please her parents, but nothing worked. She was extremely devout as a child, bicycling every Sunday morning to church which was a long way away, all by herself. God did not save her from her parents. Her husband was remorselessly cold and critical, never ceasing to remark on her shortcomings. It is important to add that she never stopped trying: she kept trying to please her family, God, her husband. She worked hard in her life in the world, had an advanced degree, a good job, and was published in several scholarly publications. In this dream, Heather asks God for comfort and it comes immediately, covered with symbols of richness and bounty. This is exactly what she needed as healing for her life's difficulties. Richness and bounty in her relationship with God, richness and bounty in her relationship with others, appreciation for her many gifts. Interestingly, not long after this, she met someone who fell deeply in love with her and admired her particularly for the qualities that were unique to her: her mind, her wonderful sense of humor, her love of life in spite of adversity. Her child recovered and began to thrive and her life became indeed filled with bounty. We can see that this dream has a number of features: it is, in itself, comforting. It holds the image of comfort to come. It suggests that comfort is available by asking. Heather is finally allowed to lie down and stop trying so hard. It demonstrates many of the features of relationship with God that appear in every major religious tradition. The divine is dependable, comforting, and upholding. We don't have to do it all, God will provide. God is responsive. It also calls to mind images from the New Testament about unnecessary anxiety.[1] This was quite new for Heather. It contradicted her ego-based picture of the world, replacing it with an image from the Self's standpoint. From the Self's standpoint, comfort and bounty were both available. It is important to note that what Heather needed from the Self was a sense of being supported. From the ego's point of view, her difficulties were not around too much ego strength and confidence, but not enough. Her sense of herself had become very eroded, and the Self supplemented it.

All the features of the dream I've mentioned so far fall into the category of positive qualities. There is fulfillment of the ego's desire for comfort, there is possibility in the symbols of richness and plenty, there is a positive relation between the ego and the Self in that the Self is responsive to the ego's needs. However, in every dream, if only by implication, there is a darker side. I will specifically mention the darker sides of these healing dreams because they are often not attended to as they are in other dreams. The darker side of this dream is presented through the very images of comfort. If Heather is not able to use the Self's nourishment to help her regain ego strength, and move out of a longing for comfort from God and into a relation in which she is able to submit her ego to the difficulties a relation with the divine creates—if she cannot move from lying down to standing up—she will not grow spiritually. This dream is a dream of Heather as God's child. Many people get stuck here in their desire for comfort and parenting, and are unable to continue the spiritual path when it becomes more difficult and painful, which it inevitably does. A sense of God as the source of comfort and bounty can be a distraction from the fact that a relation to God or Self challenges the realities and priorities of the ego and ultimately restructures them so that they are sometimes radically different from their original forms. "Home truths" that seemed unchangeable can be turned upside down. Unless one is willing to submit to this, spiritual life will not progress. If we are lucky, the experience of submission can also be an experience of relief, finally acknowledging that what we suspected is true: the ego is not in charge and is not meant to be in charge.

This next dream is a dream of comfort of a different kind. The dreamer is not suffering deeply, but is dealing with a problem she doesn't know how to solve. The dreamer is a child of about seven. She is not a client, but a member of my extended family. She comes from a solid Southern Baptist background, with parents who are kind but who have set strongly defined behavioral and moral standards for their children and themselves. Her mother, by her own admission, was especially fussy about untidiness. This is Leslie's dream.

Jesus Visits

> There is a knock at the door. I open the door, and Jesus is standing there. He says, "Can I come in?" I say, "No, it's too messy." Jesus says, "Don't worry, I'll help you clean up."

The setting of this dream seems almost certainly to be drawn from scripture. The passage from Matthew, was already familiar to Leslie because it was a favorite in the church she attended: "Ask, and it will be given to you; seek, and you will find; knock, and it will be opened. For everyone who asks receives; and he who seeks finds, and to him who knocks it will be opened."[2]

From this standpoint, it's worth noticing that it's Jesus who knocks and Leslie who opens the door. It is, spiritually, the other shoe dropping. We seek Jesus and Jesus also seeks us. There's also a reversal in their interchange: Leslie doesn't ask Jesus for anything; rather, Jesus asks if he can come in. It seems to demonstrate Leslie's fundamental understanding of our relationship to the divine: we seek God, but God also seeks us. But most importantly, for Leslie, the being that she had been taught to regard as her Lord and Savior, who died for humanity as the ultimate sacrifice, was also, unlike her mother in some experiences she had had, not annoyed by messiness while at the same time acknowledging it as a problem. He didn't reproach her, but at the same time, he wasn't indifferent. He didn't disagree with her mother's standards; he seemed to agree with her that messiness required some change, and he offered to help her himself. For Leslie, the divine is a kind, nonjudgmental helper who will help her live up to the standards she has internalized, the divine is the ideal strengthener of a child's ego, and perhaps a supplementary role model to the one she already has. If Jesus didn't find messiness terribly upsetting, maybe it wasn't the worst thing in the world. At the same time, he didn't tell her it didn't matter, which would have been very much at odds with her experience of her mother, whom she loved, admired, and saw as a role model. Jesus offered to help her with fulfilling a parental demand that she experienced as a bit beyond her, allowing her to feel that, even if she couldn't quite do what was required, it wasn't hopeless and it needn't cut her off from love and connection. It might also have reassured her that it was a small failure and not a sin. Children sometimes have difficulty in making that distinction. The most loving, understanding, knowing, and powerful being in the universe was on her side, and affirmed and would help her meet the standards of the person she loved and most wanted to please in her world. This is a comforting relation between spiritual and family authority when a child feels loved, as Leslie did.

The next dream is also a dream of comfort. This dream belongs to Jane, a client from my private practice. She is a member of the clergy, and at the time she had the dream, she was recently widowed, her father had died, and two close friends had been killed in an accident, all in the course of a month. Immediately before this series of disasters, her troubled teenaged daughter had become pregnant and had an abortion, then had fallen in love with a young man whom Jane thought was a decent person and would be kind to her daughter. This young man was then killed in an accident. Tragedy seemed to surround Jane, and even though her faith was deep, she was profoundly grief stricken, angry, and sorrowful. She was also in the awkward position of being the person who, in her small parish, had always been a comforter to others. Now she herself needed comfort, but the members of her parish were not sufficiently able to see her as a human being in order to treat her as a person in need of solace. She was depressed, wretched, and desperate, and her life energy seemed to me to be dangerously low. During this period, she had the following dream.

God as Lover of My Soul

I was in St. James' Church. I knew that in the dream, although the place didn't look at all like that church. I was sitting on the chancel platform outside the altar rail with a man. He was slim, dark haired, and attractive. I thought of him as a priest. I found being near him felt very good, but I had an inner expectation that he would be busy and would find something else he needed to do more than being with me. But he stayed with me. We had a conversation which I don't recall very clearly. It was related to the texts of prayers in the prayer book. I was finding some of them good, a bit to my surprise, and when I found that some of them were not very helpful he (to my surprise because of the context) would ruefully agree with me.

I was not especially attentive to the conversation because I was more concerned with the sensation of being near him and the fact that he wasn't bored or distracted. He seemed to have nothing more important to do and he seemed to want to be with me. We sat hip to hip and as we spoke he put his arm around me. It was not the action of a lover but of a friend or relative. Still I flinched thinking that he would be repelled by the flabbiness of my fifty-year-old body. Somehow I knew that what he felt was young, firm flesh and I realized that when he looked at me that was what he saw even though I was still a mature fifty year old. I wondered at this and I realized that when he looked at me he saw only what was good in me and that he loved me and enjoyed my presence. At one point a young pregnant woman came and knelt on the step and prayed. I expected him to leave me and go to her but he didn't. He didn't ignore her but she was not more important than me (or less important). I was full of wonder and joy.

I dreamed that I woke from my dream and I woke very slowly. My hands were beneath the blankets (still in my dream). I found I was clutching the hands of my late husband. He was irritated, though not seriously, and I soothed his irritation. Then I woke from my dream and the first words I thought were, "Was that you, God?"

Again, at least one meaning of this dream is obvious. Jane was desperately in need of love and attention, especially love and attention that didn't go away. Not only had she just experienced a number of painful losses, her role in her family of origin was the caretaker. Her mother was an odd, hostile, withdrawn woman who took no pleasure in her children and paid little attention to them. The household tasks and care of the younger children had fallen to Jane. When she was small, she was close to her father. But as she grew older and he grew more unhappy, he withdrew from her as well. In addition, she had had so much sorrow that she was beginning to feel that God had abandoned her. Thus the experience of someone who is loving and not distractable or anxious to get away is particularly important to her. Notice the detail of the appearance of the young pregnant woman who is neither more nor less important than she is. From the standpoint of external life, God is able to pay attention to us all without any diminution of love. From the internal standpoint, God/the Self is able to love both Jane as she is now and the potential in Jane, symbolized by the pregnant woman. God also sees Jane as she wishes to be seen. Even though Jane is realistic about her age and appearance, there is something about her that is still young and firm, her spirit of life. This is what has enabled her to endure the tragedies in her life without breaking down. I suspect that there is also encouragement here from God that she is still attractive, that her life as a woman is not over even though her husband has died. And finally, there is a clear representation of her holding on to her husband, and his sense that this is inappropriate. He is irritated with her, though not deeply irritated. It is natural that she should grieve and hold on, but it's time to stop. She is able to soothe him, though she does not say how. Perhaps the sense that she can again depend on God indicates that she will be able to let go of her husband.

The dark side of this dream is, again, contained in the very comfort it brings. Jane has sought comfort for her loneliness through relationships with men. Her relationship with her husband was a happy one. He was an older man who encouraged and supported her in her dreams for her life. He made it possible for her to attend seminary and introduced her to a large circle of friends. In him she found the beloved father who had emotionally withdrawn from her, the nurturing mother, and the lover. His death deprived her of what had healed some of her early wounds. This vision of God is very much along the same lines. God is an attractive young man, and her relation with God is a relation of comfort and emotional attachment. On the positive side, from a spiritual point of view this is what she has been seeking all along. As it is for all of us, the longing for the perfect love of a partner is also the longing for God. In her dream, she finally gets what she wanted. However, like Heather, she will need to move on from this image of relationship with God. This is an anthropomorphic image of God, common not only to Christians but to people from other religious traditions, in which God is represented in human terms with human qualities. The urgent need for relationship with others is the need of the ego, not the Self. A long tradition of religious solitaries and hermits attests to the fact that oneness with the divine allows us to let go of this as an urgent need, and if we think of Meister Eckhart, oneness with the divine can remove the divine completely from human form and the possibility of human attachment.[3] While I do not wish to enter into the argument about whether apophatic spirituality is superior to cataphatic spirituality, it is important not to require the divine to come in one particular form, or in a form at all.

The following dream belongs to Eleanor, an Anglican priest who was in her seventies when she had the dream. At the time of the dream she was suffering from a serious heart condition and expected to die at any time. She has since done so. The setting of the dream has two important features: she was very ill and expected to die, and her spiritual director, to whom she felt a very close connection, was also ill and unable to see her.

God in Christ

There was crowd of all kinds of people. Every ethnic group you can think of. Christ seemed to rise from behind and came

toward me above the crowd. He moved without walking. He had
the face of one of the icons that was displayed in the course on
icons given at the cathedral. He was dressed in brown in contemporary clothes, and had on a plain brown tie and a brown
suit. His face was like the icon: a black trimmed beard, black
hair, dark eyes. He didn't reach out his hand for me to take; I
thought he would, but he didn't. Right after the dream, he was
always with me even in waking life. Now, since my spiritual director has recovered and I can see her again, he comes and goes.

The first feature of this dream is its familiarity. This a dream about the
divine we can recognize. If we think of even numinous dreams as compensatory, we might want to ask why this woman, whose life has been given to
the practice of Christianity, is dreaming about Jesus. We might expect her
unconscious to send her some image that would supplement her familiar conscious beliefs. I think this dream is worth our attention because some Jungians
seem to feel that participation in a religious tradition stifles spiritual experience.
Jung himself had major personal and theoretical issues with Christianity that
inspired and informed his work. However, for many, Christianity continues to
be an extremely vibrant and meaningful religious tradition, a tradition to
which people have an experiential relation as well as a relationship of belief.
Jesus was a major figure in this woman's spiritual life; he had appeared to her
in various forms throughout her life. In this instance, the appearance of Jesus is
meaningful in a variety of ways. First of all, this is a reassuring dream about the
coming end of her relationship to the world as she knows it. Eleanor realized
she could die at any minute, and knowing that Jesus was closer was reassuring
for her. This is meaning on the existential level. The dream helps her to deal
with the nearness and inevitability of death. Then there is his rising from a
crowd of people of every ethnic background. This seems to be an image of
both universality from the existential point of view, and of her whole self from
the standpoint of inner life. This Jesus is everyone's Jesus as well as hers, her
whole self's Jesus as well as her ego's. This Jesus may also be an image of the
Self, the spiritual and organizing center of the psyche, surrounded by all the
elements of the psyche. Because she is approaching death, it seems possible that
another implication of the group is that she is about to join the mass of souls
who have gone before. It also suggests an opening of her heart with an image
that is familiar to anyone who lives in Vancouver. Vancouver has possibly the
richest ethnic mix of any city in North America. It is a condition of our lives
in Vancouver that we constantly come into contact with people very different
from ourselves. Eleanor comes from a white, upper-class English background.
The fact that Jesus comes from behind the crowd may also suggest that Jesus is
found through the love of our fellow human beings, no matter what their
ethnic background.

The image of Jesus is both old and modern. Though his face resembles the face of an early Christian icon, he is dressed in contemporary clothes: he is both old and new, both human and divine. He wears contemporary clothes, but he floats above the crowd. Interestingly, the dream also contains some disappointment: Eleanor expects him to take her hand, but he does not. His image stays with her, but they do not touch. I asked her if she thought it might be because, though she believed she would die imminently, she did not. Perhaps Christ grasping her hand would have meant to her that he was leading her out of human life. She agreed that this was a strong possibility. This interpretation would also reinforce the idea that the large number of ethnically mixed people represent souls that have moved on. But even though they do not touch, Christ is present for her.

What part did this dream play in her spiritual life? I suggest the dream had two functions. First of all, it is a reassuring dream. Though she seemed to accept her own impending death, no doubt she also had some misgivings. The dream offered her a direct experience of Christ as opposed to a theoretical belief in the afterlife, something that no one can have a direct experience of. The second was the beginning of the resolution of a powerful archetypal transference to her spiritual director. Eleanor's spiritual life had been considerably enriched by spiritual direction; it had allowed her to resolve a number of spiritual issues and experience the presence of the divine much more deeply. As a result, she had developed a strong archetypal transference to her spiritual director and to the Cathedral Centre for Spiritual Direction itself. The illness of her spiritual director allowed her to begin to shift her devotion away from her spiritual director towards its appropriate object. When her spiritual director recovered, she no longer experienced Christ as constantly present; clearly the projections that constituted the transference were not yet completely withdrawn. She seemed to be in a transitional state. Perhaps this was one reason for this dream, whose compensatory quality is not entirely obvious for a member of the Christian clergy: her love of God was at that time also partly transference to another human being, which needed to be resolved. This leads us to another feature of this dream, which it shares with all dreams about the divine: it contains the shadow side of the relationship with the divine, the part that is likely to be problematic. Jesus does not reach out to Eleanor and Eleanor does not reach out to him. Eleanor's spiritual life may have contained a passive element with respect to her relationship with the divine. Perhaps she had difficulty in reaching out to Jesus, which was partially resolved through her relationship with her spiritual director. It is also possible that this was an ongoing difficulty, an emotional as well as a spiritual holding-back.

Here are two other dreams that brought comfort, but also went beyond comfort to something new and a change in the relation of ego to Self. In these dreams, the dreamer has transforming experiences that are also healing.

These dreams belong to Laura, a woman who has had a painful and difficult life with many losses, and who had recently undergone a long and serious illness. The following account includes both the dreams and Laura's commentary on her dreams.

Renewal in Christ: Encounters

> I was living with my nine-year-old daughter in a graceful Victorian house. I saw a young boy in nineteenth-century clothing standing in a doorway, smiling at me; then he turned and disappeared. I asked my daughter about him, and she said that he was a ghost. In fact, she had seen many ghosts in the house. I looked up and saw the ghosts, too—some were frightening, ragged-looking wraiths. I took my daughter by the hand and we ran out into the garden.
>
> There we found a beautiful young man (who looked like a serene Kurt Cobain) sitting with his back against a low stone wall. He explained that my daughter and I were also ghosts. I suddenly knew that this was my home, and my daughter and I could live in the house with the young man. We would be a family.
>
> Just then, my ex-lover came walking up the path. I chose to take on the form of a mildewed apparition to frighten him away. I was both inside myself and watching the dream like a movie, so I shocked myself awake.

As a person who has always been profoundly horrified by the thought of ghosts, I am surprised by my lack of terror in this dream. I felt uneasy inside the ghost house, but in the garden with the young man, I felt something more like awe. I experienced an expansion of my world—one where the ghostly realm was included.[4] *Along with my bewilderment was a growing sense of excitement: there was a whole new world to explore. And in that world I had a husband and my daughter had a father. I had a profound feeling of belonging. That same night I dreamt:*

> I was swimming in a small reedy pond. I noticed a gap in the bulrushes that was almost like a door or gate. I peeked through the opening.
>
> On the other side was a huge, placid lake I hadn't known was there. An enormous black fish came swimming toward me, looming larger and larger. It was definitely a fish, but it was so huge it swam with its body half way out of the water, like a child's drawing of a whale.
>
> I pulled back, but the fish was coming so quickly, I had no time to do anything. The fish came through the "doorway" and swam up to me and around me. I looked up at it, filled with a

powerful feeling of awe. As before, I felt a breathtaking fear more akin to excitement than menace. The black fish was simply an overwhelming presence.

I believe these two "companion" dreams have the same theme, and that the second illuminates the first. The "black fish" is a Christian symbol for me, representing the (dark, unknowable) mystery that is Christ. I believe that the young man in the garden (Kurt Cobain—that volatile fusion of creativity and suffering) is also Jesus.

In both dreams, I encounter a realm beyond what is known to me—a place of spirit where I am welcomed, even sought after—a world I am meant to inhabit.

Laura and I have worked together for many years, and her life has been exceptionally difficult. She has a history of painful, conflicted, and generally unsatisfying relationships, beginning with her parents. She is a single parent, and is recovering from a long illness complicated by depression. One of Laura's coping mechanisms throughout her life has been making massive efforts to get things to go well. This includes her relationships, where she assumed responsibility for making her partner happy, and work, where her willingness to work extremely hard in order to feel like part of the company "family" was exploited to the point where she finally had to take sick leave because she was so exhausted. After she did so, it was discovered that she has an immune disorder that is potentially serious. She is now on disability, and is retraining for another, less stressful job.

Laura's capacity for effort has worked both for and against her. The ways in which it has worked against her I have mentioned above. The ways in which it has worked for her are now beginning to emerge more clearly. While it is true that her persistence kept her in relationships and job situations that harmed her, it is also true that she was able to look for help until she found it. She has worked hard in therapy, and she has sought and found help when things between her and her daughter were not going well. She energetically looked for some kind of work that she could do, even though she never feels really well and it would be possible for her to remain on disability for the rest of her life. Her religious background is Catholic, but the Catholic Church was never a good fit for her. Her overdeveloped sense of personal responsibility combined with her religious instruction to make her feel guilty all the time about virtually everything, which kept her trying harder and harder. Nevertheless, she did not give up on having a spiritual life, or even on Christianity. She kept trying until she found a church in which she felt comfortable, and there her spiritual life blossomed. One of Laura's most significant areas of growth has been the development of a sense of balance: along with her capacity to keep trying until she finds what she needs, she has developed the ability to trust that life can bring her what she wants and needs without her having to try all the time. Both of these dreams involve discovery rather than effort: she finds herself in the house of ghosts, she discovers the placid lake where the black fish lives. In order to do this, Laura first had to push herself to her limits, to finally discover that trying didn't work and she was literally unable to try any harder. Illness prevented her from continuing to drive herself to meet the unreasonable demands made on her at work, and her last relationship was so chaotic, demanding, and draining that she found it impossible to go on. Finally, she was able to give up. Now, having been virtually incapacitated for more than two years, feeling that there might be nothing for her in life, she has begun to reemerge from this painful period of her life, and as well from the darkness emanating from her depressed, angry, and demanding parents that surrounded her from childhood and which she had internalized. She is reentering life, not as the flawed-feeling little girl who was never good enough, but as her real self. This is the first time in her life she has been without a relationship with a partner, but she feels that has enabled her to deepen her relationship with her daughter. She is and always will be a hard worker, but she takes care of herself and respects her own limits. She has experienced a spiritual renewal, enjoying and appreciating life as never before, and able to trust in God to bring her what she needs. Remembering Corbett's view that the divine enters the psyche through the most wounded place, the divine entered Laura's psyche through a nearly complete collapse, when she had to admit that, no matter how hard she tried, she couldn't force anyone to love her or her employers to appreciate her. I have worked with many clients who have experienced spiritual growth through difficulties in life, but Laura stands out both from the standpoint of how much she has lost, and how radically she has been transformed. Her life is an especially vivid example of two of Jesus's descriptions of the spiritual life:

> Anyone who wants to be a follower of mine must renounce self; he must take up his cross and follow me. Whoever wants to save his life will lose it, but whoever loses his life for my sake and for the gospel's will save it. What does anyone gain by winning the whole world at the cost of his life? What can he give to buy his life back?[5]

> So I say to you, ask, and you will receive; seek, and you will find; knock, and the door will be opened to you. For everyone who asks receives, those who seek find, and to those who knock, the door will be opened.[6]

These passages from the New Testament describe two important aspects of spiritual life. First, there is the necessity of loss. We must give up on the ego's version of life in order to flourish spiritually, to have new life. At first

Laura was profoundly unwilling to give up. She tried and tried until she was both physically ravaged and emotionally desperate. She was finally forced to give up because she couldn't go on as she was. When she did give up, she became much more open to the life of the spirit, and rediscovered her Christianity through connecting it with the inner life and real spiritual experiences. As a result of this, she is emerging as her true self, and not the anxious-to-please, self-disregarding person she was forced into becoming as a child.

Second, it is important to persist. In order that a door be opened, we must knock. I have always thought that the apparently cynical saying "God helps those who help themselves" actually contains an important insight into spiritual and even everyday life. Unless we make some sort of effort, nothing happens. In spiritual life, we must make an effort to connect with the divine through spiritual practice and seeking a religious community. In everyday life, we must look for possibilities, actively engage in life. Whatever our relation to the divine, the divine will not live our lives for us. However, if we are active in our own lives without insisting on the ego's point of view, help will come from a deeper source. This is just what happened to Laura. I have known few people, either as clients or as friends, who have tried to improve their lives as much as Laura has. Once she could face reality, understanding what was worth trying for and what wasn't, her ability to make a great deal of effort stopped being dangerous to her and instead became an important aspect of a strong character. She had always had what I would call a good character: she was and is kind, benevolent, brave, loyal, and truthful. Now her ability to exercise self-discipline and make efforts has enabled her to engage with life in a discerning way, discovering both what makes her happy and her authentic relation to the divine. The same day she told me the two dreams above, she told me this is the happiest she has ever been.

The last dream belong to Sean, an experienced and well-respected therapist who also has an active and long-standing spiritual life involving the practice of meditation. He has experienced some health and family difficulties in his life in recent years but has been able to deal with them, and throughout them has had a regular spiritual practice and worked with his dreams. Recently he had the following dream. His own comments follow.

Flying Fish

I am in some semi-tropical place where a river flows into the ocean. It is a beautiful warm, sunny day. I am walking along a road by the river and notice huge fish in the crystal clear water. Some seem to be squid and then later I see manta rays. They are fascinating and beautiful. Along the shoreline of the ocean, someone points out the water rippling as thousand of little fish swarm. All of a sudden they start flying out of the water—they are little sailfish. One of them, however, turns out to be huge; it is multicolored and after leaping high out of the water it lands near me so I get a good look at it. I am going to meet some people and can't wait to tell them what I've seen. I also feel sorry for them that they've missed it.

The dream was extremely vivid, in "technicolor" and had a magical quality. I was filled with a sense of how special the world is; its beauty can be unexpected and breathtaking. There was also a transcendent quality. I didn't have to do anything in the dream; everything just unfolded in front of me. I practice meditation and the dream seemed to capture the experience of really being present.

This beautiful imagery suggests that Sean is witnessing the place where the ego meets the Self, "where a river flows into the ocean." He is able to see into the divine, but in a special way: he can see both the beauty of the world and the beauty of the divine. Though the presence of fish often suggest a sense of depth, there is not so much a sense of depth here as a sense of nearness, of transparency. The divine is near, is here close to us. The flying fish leaps out of the water right in front of Sean, he walking right by the river, and everything unfolds before him. He doesn't have to do anything. There is a strong sense of grace, of the revelation of the beauty and wonder of the world. There is also a strong sense, as he says, of presence. Everything is full of being. Fish, which are usually invisible in the depths, are fully visible on the surface and even in the air. There are many kinds; they are colorful, fascinating, and beautiful. They can swim and they can fly. They have all sorts of shapes. There's a sense of bounty. To put it in psychic terms, a multiplicity of divine beings is flying up from the unconscious; it's an image of mystical experience that is not anthropomorphic, yet it's still cataphatic. As well, there's an angelic quality to these fish yet they're still fish. We need neither eliminate nature and move to the void, nor do we need to turn nature into something other than itself to experience the divine.

Sean's dream seems to be a dream of Being, cataphatic rather than apophatic,[7] nevertheless Being. It demands nothing, yet it gives everything. The experience is transcendent, the beauty is breathtaking. Perhaps the flying fish is the Self glimpsed for just a moment in its divine play. No wonder Sean feels sorry for those who missed it!

Looking at the dreams in this chapter, some themes emerge. Heather's and Jane's dreams represent healing as healing of the ego, or the concerns of the conscious self. Both of these women had experienced so much suffering that their conscious sense of self was in serious danger of collapse. These very positive experiences of the divine brought with them an increased sense of strength and life that endured. Heather bought a comforter that resembled the one in her dream, making the divine a constant presence in her waking life. Jane was able to let go of her husband and move into new life. Though both of these women continued to struggle with life's difficulties, neither felt so alone.

A healthy ego plays an important part in spiritual life. We need a strong but not rigid ego to support us through the inevitable trials of life and the inner turbulence that invariably accompanies emotional and spiritual growth. While it is true that, ultimately, the ego-Self axis or relationship with the divine requires the ego to give up its supremacy, it also makes the ego stronger and more flexible. The ego is no longer in competition with Self for control, but can be sustained and nourished (as well as challenged) by the Self. The relation of ego and Self is curiously like our relation to other people. One of the greatest anxieties I have encountered in clients is the anxiety that, if the divine should actually be experienced, the person who has such experiences will go mad, become depersonalized, split off from reality, and never successfully find her or his way back. People who feel these anxieties most profoundly are those whose relations with their parents and other caregivers have been coercive and controlling. There is a strong correlation between our original experiences of care and our expectations of the divine. These anxieties are not limited to inrushes of the divine during meditation, contemplation, and/or prayer. They also gather around everyday experience of the divine; people who feel these anxieties do not trust their own intuitions and ideas that "just come to them," do not have confidence in their own ability to manage life's difficulties (referring to Jung's notion of the divine as "anything that gets in my way"), and often have very cynical attitudes towards any form of organized religion.

Eleanor was at a very different point in her life. She was about to leave a long and eventful life, and she needed reassurance that the faith that had meant so much to her was real, that she really could trust Jesus and forget about her somewhat rigid upbringing and her fear of death, and finally transfer her love of her spiritual director, whom she would have to leave behind, to God. The dream does not entirely answer these questions. Eleanor and Jesus do not touch, yet there is a strong sense of connection. Eleanor seems prepared to love her fellow human beings as Jesus did, and she seems able to experience Jesus as a part of life—a man in a suit, not an idealized being in a white robe and a halo. The dream meant a great deal to Eleanor, and soon after she died at peace.

Laura's dreams are not about the healing of the ego, though that has been one effect of her work. The dreams are about discovering the reality of the divine and the expansive effect this has on our sense of both the realities and possibilities of life. Laura discovered a whole other world that she had previously feared. I suspect the frightening aspect of the spirits comes from the frightening, depriving picture of spiritual life she developed from the grim version of Catholicism she learned as a child. This spirit world[7] is a world where she can have what she needs, including a husband and a father for her daughter. Christ, in the guise of Kurt Cobain, is the companion she's always wanted. She recognizes her heart's desire, and even drives away an ex-lover, who in real life was both selfish and callous. He may also represent a whole way of life she's rejecting—trying to please men, giving them an infinite number of chances, overriding her own sorrow to cling to relationships that weren't working. In the dream about the fish, she begins by swimming in a pond and discovers both a large lake she didn't know was there and a beautiful, mysterious, and awe-inspiring fish, an ancient Christian symbol. She is part of a much bigger world than the small pond of her ego's point of view. The fish shows her another aspect of the spiritual life: not only is the divine present in a recognizable human being, it also has other forms of existence, less familiar and domestic. It is large, it is black, it comes from the depths. However, she is not frightened or in any way put off by this more impersonal representation of the divine. She experiences awe and wonder, and these feelings have stayed with her. These are truly dreams of spiritual transformation. There is transformation within the dreams: she is not afraid of the ghost house and recognizes that this is what she really needs, she discovers a part of the lake she didn't know was there, and the wonderful being that emerges from it fills her with awe and wonder. There has also been transformation in her waking life, as she moves from the loneliness, frustration, and exhaustion of her earlier life to the deep happiness, capacity for joy, and ability to truly love God, her daughter, and herself in her present life.

Finally, Sean's dream affirmed his sense of the divine as experienced through full presence in the moment. It was this kind of experience that meditation pointed him toward, and the dream offered him an experience of presence in the moment, and of transcendent and transforming beauty that is at the heart of the divine. The only shadow element present in Sean's dream was his selfless regret that his friends had missed it.

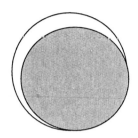

5
Dreams of Energy

The divine can be experienced in dreams as an increase in and intensification of energy. This can be experienced as inspiring and enhancing or threatening, depending on the attitude of the dreamer to involuntary increases in energy. In the last chapter, I talked about the fact that many people feel frightened and threatened by experiences of the divine. This is not the kind of awe that is characteristic of numinous experiences, but is rather apprehensive fear, the fear that the experience of the divine might set off some kind of psychic catastrophe. The specifics of the feared psychic catastrophes vary, but some common versions are the fear of splitting off from reality and entering some altered state of consciousness from which it is impossible to return, the fear of the shattering of personality resulting in the inability to function, and the fear of becoming an obsessive religious fanatic. These anxieties are often connected with a strong need for control of experience because of powerful and painful repressed emotions in unconscious complexes. For people who do not have these fears, experiencing the divine as a form of energy can increase psychic liveliness and intensify the experience of everyday life.

The two following dreams are examples of the experience of the divine as an increase in energy. Both dreamers are women who live their lives with enthusiasm and zest, and who do not fear spontaneous incursions of energy.

Roxanne is a bisexual artist whose art is largely concerned with sexuality and its manifestations. Vancouver is a city tolerant of sexual diversity, and as a result, Roxanne has access to and spends time with drag queens, transvestites, transsexuals, and every other imaginable sexual variation. These images all make their way into her art. Though of English background and brought up as an Anglican, neither Christianity nor traditional values play a great part in her life. She is not connected with any spiritual tradition, but values that I would call spiritual play an important part in her life. She has a love of life, an acceptance of others, kindness of heart, and above all an optimism that is quite unusual. She describes herself as having no guilt about her unusual lifestyle, something which is partly due to her family's complete acceptance of her choices which no doubt has contributed to her strong sense of self-possession. She has very few fixed notions about how people should live apart from ethical ones. She came for therapy because several friends of hers were clients of mine, and she needed someone to reflect with. She felt she was going through a transition in her life that had to do with living more fully, believing more deeply in her own work, and getting over a reticence about expecting to earn a decent living from her work. She was generous with others, but was not at all good at asking for what she needed for herself, especially financially. She had recently ended a difficult relationship with someone who was psychologically troubled, demanding, and self-absorbed. She felt there was some block she needed to remove in order to enter more fully and pleasurably into her own life. After we had been working together for about a year, she had the following dream.

The Building in the Valley

> There are no people, and the feeling is one of calm and peace. The colors and light are rich with subdued shades of deep green and grey. A large, grey, three-storied institutional-style building sits nestled in a deep green lush valley. The building has banks of multipaned windows. There is a close-up of a stone/cement wall, topped with wrought iron railings. Somehow a small piece of the top of the wall chips or falls away. At this point, seen again from the first view of the building, waterfalls of white water pour simultaneously from all the windows. The feeling is one of bounty.
> I've been playing this loop over and over in my mind, and it makes me feel great with a certain richness of spirit.

Roxanne took great pleasure in this dream, and at the same time was completely bewildered by it. She experienced it as profoundly numinous, but could not place it either in her personal life or spiritually. She does not have a commitment to any religious tradition, so this area of interpretation was closed to her.

When Roxanne told me her dream, my first associations were biblical and Christian:

> Then afterward I will pour out my spirit on all flesh; your sons and your daughters shall prophesy, your old men shall dream dreams, and your young men shall see visions. Even on the male and female slaves, in those days, I will pour out my spirit. (Joel 2:28)

> The Book of Common Prayer, collect from the sixth Sunday after Trinity: O God, who has prepared for them that love thee such good things as pass man's understanding; Pour into our hearts such love toward thee, that we, loving thee above all things, may obtain thy promises, which exceed all that we can desire.[1]

> *The Book of Alternative Services*, Eucharistic Prayer #4: Pour out your spirit on the whole earth and make it your new creation.[2]

I was somewhat surprised by these associations, which were so explicitly Christian while Roxanne was not. I was sufficiently hesitant not to share them with her while she puzzled over the dream, which she found very affecting but hard to analyze. Finally I shared my thoughts, and she enthusiastically accepted them as relevant. She had, after all, an Anglican upbringing. What is particularly interesting about Roxanne's dream is the source of the divine spirit: a building that has a kind of institutional and industrial quality. Roxanne did not want to analyze this dream at great length since it had such affective power, so the following are my own speculations.

Roxanne's religious upbringing was too limiting for her—perhaps it felt like a drab building, the church and its representation of God institutional and unfeeling. Yet early religious training gives us the inner structure for later religious development. We might also see the building as an image of Roxanne's ego structure: a sturdy, serviceable building with many windows, but too contained. While her life was very unusual, it's also true that she had a great deal of difficulty in expressing her feelings; she was the child in her family who was supposed to be the mature one, responsible for another child who was ill, to not complain and be self-contained. She was entirely successful in being this sort of person not only as a child but also as an adult. She was also not supposed to want anything for herself. There is a wall around the building, and it is a change in the wall that brings the water pouring out. Two changes in her life resulted from our work together. She was much more expressive in her emotional life and, connected with this, she was much clearer about what she wanted, including what she wanted for herself in her financial life. She had always regarded financial issues as vulgar and beneath her, not connecting them with the practicalities of her life, being able to afford, for example, a computer to use creatively in the artistic life which meant so much to her. A change in this attitude seemed, in real life, to bring real bounty into her life and gave her a different feeling about herself and her life. Again, Lionel Corbett's point in *The Religious Function of the Psyche* is appropriate. The numinous enters the psyche through the wounded aspects of the psyche. Though issues of money and practicality may not seem to be deep issues, nonetheless they were deep for Roxanne, connecting with her sense of entitlement to her own feelings and desires. One of her sisters had a chronic illness and because of this, the family had had to give up an affluent lifestyle in another country to return to Canada where medical care is available to everyone. They never were able to return to the lifestyle with which she was familiar, and instead lived very frugally. Her role in the family was to be the one who was "all right," who didn't ask much for herself. Allowing herself to want things for herself and not step aside or be helpful was a profound change in attitude for her. The change, in the dream, was apparently a small change: a small chip or piece of the wall falls away. This is enough to release the bounty and "flow" in the building. The building had windows, but no apparent openings. But when the water comes, it creates its own opening. It comes out all the windows, pouring out. The building acts as a source and a container for the bounty that comes pouring out. Roxanne's ego, previously solid though filled with windows, is now permeated with the rushing waters of the divine. It was not a rigid ego, but rather one that was strong and perhaps too self-sufficient. But there is more to Roxanne than that. The lush valley may represent the larger psyche, watered by the bountiful water of the divine. Interestingly, not long after she had this dream, Roxanne was traveling and found herself in a valley exactly like the valley in her dream. There is also an existential aspect to this: Roxanne has indeed experienced increased bounty in her life, and has a strong sense of her needs being met. She has recently received awards for her work, and her artistic career is flourishing as never before.

We also need to ask ourselves where the shadow is in this dream. It seems to lie in the "closed" quality of both the building and the fence around the property. As I mentioned above, Roxanne struggles with a holding-in of affect. Roxanne is in fact quite self-contained and has a history of also containing her demands of others. This would suggest, if not a diminishing of experienced affect, a diminishing of expressed affect, which can have an impact on experienced affect. Corbett points out the affect is the bodily manifestation of the incarnation of spirit, the personal incarnation of archetypal material. Thus Roxanne may have to pay particular attention to her own capacity for expressiveness which creates, so to speak, the path for the divine. Water is a common image for feeling in dreams, so that there is both an image of frustration and a promise of release in this dream. Roxanne's dream makes me think of many passages from the book of Isaiah, which contains images of the pouring out of water and spirit, the preparing of paths but also of frustration and limitation.

This next dream belongs to Martha, one of my clients in spiritual direction. She originally came to me because she experienced herself as being in spiritual crisis. Highly successful in the business world, she was becoming more and more dissatisfied with her life. When she came to see me, she was considering quitting her job and starting theology school, but had the sense that this might be a compensatory fantasy. Her family background was small town and conservative, and her mother, who came from a lower social class than her father, was highly identified with Martha, highly critical and determined that Martha should be successful. Though Martha has been successful beyond her mother's wildest dreams, including being happily married to an equally successful businessman, nothing has ever been quite good enough for her, and she has never ceased criticizing Martha and trying to control her.

Martha had this dream as she was moving towards a solution to her crisis. In the process of telling me this dream, she mentioned that she had been having three or four nightmares a week for some time, and asked me if that was unusual. This gives a sense of the acuteness of her crisis.

God, the Jaguar

> I dreamt that I was on safari with my family. We were in a jeep and the game people were told to chase animals towards us, although we did not know that they were being chased in our direction. We were disappointed to find that out later. We saw bears and cougars and some other animals. All of a sudden, a beautiful iridescent purple and green jaguar arrives. The person sitting next to me rolls down the window to get a look at this amazing animal. The cat jumps in through the window and comes for me. I am saved by the man sitting next to me and my father who get it off of me. The person beside me gets a scratch. My father takes off a paw. The cat is killed when one of the guides breaks its neck. It is horrible to see it dead because it was so beautiful and magical alive.

This seems to be a dream about the violent incursion of the divine. The most prominent level of the dream initially seems to be the inner level. She is indeed with her family psychically, still sharing their values, driving through territory filled with wild animals in a closed car. The game people are told to chase animals towards them—this is an ambiguous aspect of the dream. It may have to do with her inheritance of her parents' picture of life as being controllable. From one standpoint, it makes the appearance of the game somewhat artificial rather than natural, and this is reinforced by their disappointment when they find out. However, from another standpoint, the game people and whoever has been told to chase the animals towards them may be a disowned wish, a desire to have more wild animals in her life. Suddenly the disowned wish comes true: a beautiful iridescent purple and green jaguar jumps through the window and specifically comes for Martha. This wild magical energy is experienced as dangerous. Her father takes off a paw and the animal is killed. She is horrified by its death, since it was so beautiful and magical alive. The jaguar seems to represent her own possibility of embodiment of the divine.[3] But it is so at odds with her current life situation that she experiences it as dangerous, possibly even lethal. But the alternative, killing it, is also utterly horrible. This conflict seemed to be one of the sources of Martha's nightmares. The alternatives in the dream are death or despair.

Martha's deeper nature appeared to be at odds with the way she had been living her life. She lived an extremely structured life which was focused on activities that are connected with the traditional and archetypal masculine—achievement in business, the cultivation of objectivity, and intellectual activity. Perhaps this masculine identification was represented by her father in the dream, who tears a paw off the magical jaguar. Her spiritual life is Christian: she has been an Anglican since childhood, and experiences the liturgy and corporate worship very profoundly. But there is something more to Martha than the faith of her childhood. My sense of this is that it is not just that the imagery of Christianity is not adequate for her, but also Christianity is the familiar and the known. Even though her Christianity is very strong, she needs to step outside this frame of reference to deepen her contact with the divine. There is a strong sense of containment in the dream—the closed car—that requires the divine to come to her. One thinks here of Saint Paul and his violent experience of the divine. Martha's experience of the divine is so violent that the cat has to be killed. Another interesting feature of Martha's dream is that the image of the divine is so determined to get to her that it risks its life and dies for her. We don't know whether it actually intended to harm her, or whether it was willing to die in order to terrify her into awe.

Martha's dream illustrates a situation that is frequently found with people who have spiritual commitments that are habitual: in order to deepen their faith, they need to be willing to admit imagery and experiences that are not familiar or even apparently consistent with their existing faith. Many people have strong anxieties about orthodoxy, about admitting to consciousness material that threatens the beliefs they already have. They need to be able to accept spiritual experiences they do not understand and "hold" them, not attempting to tailor them to fit their existing views. This is especially true for Christians, so many of whom center religious experience around strong ethical prescriptions and prohibitions.[4] Martha was in a particularly good position to do this; her childhood faith had not until recently played a prominent role in her adult life nor had her family endorsed a view of the world that was religiously rigid, so she was not threatened by an experience that seemed outside religious borders. The ability to admit strange and even incomprehensible imagery and experience seems to be partly a function of the flexibility of the ego, and the extent to which the ego is identified with a particular tradition or approach. We all know people who would describe themselves as "good Christians"—such people seem to have more difficulty than someone like Martha, who views life and herself as being in constant process. In fact Martha makes an excellent example of someone who is able to tolerate various sources of meaning: rational, intuitive, mystical. This dream was very upsetting to Martha, but she was able to remember it. This is a dark dream, with the divine appearing violently and being killed by the powerful patriarchal spirit by which Martha lived her life. Nevertheless it has made its appearance. Martha has shown a tendency to successfully repress importance aspects of her being to the point of creating violent and apparently potentially dangerous conflict; she came to me partly because of the many nightmares she had been having. She is currently struggling with this, and it may be something she will have to contend with throughout her life: she has a powerful, logical mind and a strong practical bent. The difficulties Jung referred to in "The Transcendent Function," that modern life requires us to cut ourselves off from the unconscious and resist unconscious material breaking through, are particularly applicable here.[5] Martha will need to pay particular attention to the ease with which she is able to do what is expected, take care of business, make the practical choice rather than follow her heart. However, her struggles have been effective. Her life now resembles much more the life she wants. She is a strong and determined person, able to carry her conflicts.

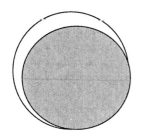

6

Bad Dreams about the Divine

When we think about dreams that take us beyond the ego, we usually think of dreams that involve feelings of awe, of love, of wonder, dreams that leave us with a sense of being changed for the better or even healed of some wound or suffering. Many numinous dreams are indeed of this kind. However, the process of individuation and the spiritual journey involve fear and suffering as well as wonder and joy. This is clear from the work of Jung and from the writings of the mystics. To come into relation with the Self/divine involves a challenge to the illusory supremacy of the ego. Though it is an illusion, it is one of the ego's favorite illusions, partly because, in the first half of life, it is essential. As Jung pointed out in "The Transcendent Function," in order to manage in the kind of complex external world in which we find ourselves, we are strongly identified with the ego and often experientially sealed off from the unconscious. Thus any kind of influx of unconscious or divine energy can create a sense of fear and disturbance. If the Self/divine is particularly exigent, we can feel overwhelmed. Furthermore, to experience the divine in ourselves is not an unambiguous pleasure. As we will see, one aspect of having strong contact with the divine is an awareness of the suffering of the world and a desire to do good. Because of our limitations, this is not always possible. In Charles Dickens's *A Christmas Carol*, Marley's ghost presents us with an image of our longing to help those who are rigid, angry, and unhappy, and the necessity of the intervention of the divine in order to do so. Our awareness that it is not possible through an effort of will does not cause our desire to do so to disappear. We continue to participate in the suffering of those we cannot help, and at best it sometimes seems that our participation, especially through prayer, can help bring more divine energy into their lives. In this chapter, I want to discuss two dreams that, from the dreamers' point of view, were "bad" dreams. That is, they did not leave the dreamers feeling inspired and changed for the better. Rather, they left the dreamers in a state of disturbance. Both of these dreams had lasting effects on the dreamers and demonstrate aspects of the spiritual journey.[1]

The first dream is a dream that I had when I was training as a spiritual director. It is a dark and disturbing dream, and illustrates, among other things, the intensity of the pressure from the Self as the ego-Self axis is strengthening or, to put it another way, the difficulty of actually putting oneself in the hands of the living God.

A Dark and Terrible Sound

> War has broken out and I have been drafted. I'm in uniform, and I'm going to the Hotel Vancouver, the embarcation point. It is night, absolutely black with the exception of a small door on the side of the hotel, where there is light shining through. Then I am inside. All the halls are dark and there are pools of water on the floor where there are others sleeping. Then there is a loud clattering sound which is so powerful I have a sense it penetrates my body completely—there is no sense of "hearing" it—it gets into me. I run down a spiral staircase getting deeper and deeper—there is a tremendous sense of motion. I feel overwhelmed.

Let us begin by asking why this constitutes a dream about the divine. First, it was a numinous dream though not pleasantly numinous. It clearly had the feel of being about something beyond myself, a characteristic that is represented by the images of the dream. Second, the subject matter of the dream is the overcoming of the ego by a force greater than itself. The sound that reverberates through the dream, penetrating everything including the dreamer's body, is a powerful representation of the power of the divine that knows no barriers. Ordinarily, the body's boundaries are distinct. Unless some weapon is used, we do not penetrate the boundaries of the bodies of others except by natural means, such as feeding and sex. But the sound in this dream penetrates and saturates the body with no regard for its boundaries. It penetrates everything and everywhere, and its effect is to drive the dreamer deeper, down the spiral stairs deeper into the psyche. However, this representation of the psyche is not a pleasant one. It is dark, grey, full of pools, perhaps pools of sorrow. There is no comfort anywhere, only stark, damp surroundings and virtually unbearable noise. Nevertheless, the dreamer does not run out the door, a door we have seen in the first scene of the dream. The dreamer goes deeper, running down the spiral stairs. This is a classic dream of confrontation between the Self and the ego. Without a spiritual perspective, we might classify this as a bad dream because of its unpleasantness. With a spiritual perspective, such dreams can be dreams of great depth. They present the demands of the Self for giving up the ego's control. They represent the ego's fear of doing this, and the threatening quality of spiritual life from the ego's standpoint.

This is a very different vision of the divine from that of God as comforter or lover of my soul. The dream represents the sacrificial nature of spiritual life, but it represents it not as sacrifice (because we don't see a transforming outcome) but as loss. The difference between sacrifice and loss is an important difference from both a Jungian and a more exclusively spiritual standpoint. Both the Christian tradition and Jung offer us the notion of the *felix culpa*, the fortunate fall or happy fault (the literal meaning), the bad thing that happens that turns out not just to bring good things but better, transformative things. From this standpoint, some of the unwelcome things that happen in life fall into the category of the *felix culpa*. We lose a job we're attached to but that is not fulfilling. We grieve, then find a job that we love, but wouldn't have sought if we hadn't lost the first one. From an interior standpoint, we may be very attached to a certain way of looking at the world that we are forcibly deprived of. Perhaps we had very good parents and as a result believe that all people are good at heart given enough time and love. Then something happens that is disillusioning: someone betrays us, or we come into contact with someone who has allied her or himself with the dark side of her or his nature and actively wants to harm us. The disillusionment is painful, but the transformation provides additional depth and breadth to the ego's picture of life. We become aware that life is full of both good and evil, and demands discernment rather than a naive innocence. From both a Jungian and a Christian standpoint, the story of the Fall is the story of a *felix culpa*. From a Jungian perspective, it results in the birth of consciousness. Before the fall, Adam and Eve did not experience themselves as separate from the divine, nor did either of them have a sense of autonomy. Like all increases of consciousness, this one was dearly bought, and, from a Christian point of view, was the beginning of a long series of events which culminated in the Incarnation, a *felix culpa* indeed.

Most sacred texts offer examples of loss turned into sacrifice. Perhaps the ultimate example in Christian text is Christ's crucifixion. Jesus prayed in the Garden of Gethsemane to allow the cup of crucifixion to pass from him. From his point of view as a human being, it was an absolute loss. He would lose his life and die in excruciating pain. The text of the crisis in the garden is exclusively concerned with the struggle between the human and the divine, between the perspective of loss and the perspective of sacrifice. Sacrifice is transforming. Through sacrifice we become more than we were, more deeply rooted in the divine, and ego gains more access to the Self. One of the most difficult and essential tasks in spiritual life is to come to understand our losses as sacrifices, as doing the will of the divine. That opposes our natural inclination, which is to see them as losses.

In this dream, I am being changed from a soldier answering a call to arms, a call represented by my wearing my father's army uniform. I have been drafted into the masculine life, into some sort of identity-consuming aggressive uniformity. This imagery is a reference to the way in which I had experienced many aspects of my professional life as well personal life, in particular my strong identity with my father and my sense of living, as my father did, from the head rather than the heart. As well, it reflects a sense I have often had of life as a dangerous struggle in the dark. However, once inside the building where the troops are supposed to meet to march off to war, I find myself virtually alone. The other people present appear to be sleeping. This seems to be a reference to Jesus's experience in the garden: while he was engaged in intense spiritual struggle, his companions fell asleep. It also refers to sleeping parts of the psyche, areas of unconsciousness and underdevelopment: perhaps if these people woke up, they could be of help to me. It also suggests an identification with the path of Jesus. I experience a tremendous, penetrating noise. The Self has become impatient with the ego's resistance; we might call it the wrath of God, the thundering and clattering of the demand for wholeness and the relinquishing of ego control. I have two options. I can go out the way I came, or I can go deeper. My experience of this is not a conscious experience of choice, nevertheless in every action there is a measure of choice. I seem compelled to go deeper. Perhaps the choices I have made up to that time account for the fact that I do not even look for the exit. I experience myself as running from the noise by going deeper to escape the noise. This is true to the situation in which I find myself; the only way to experience the relation to the Self/divine as something other than a negative and threatening experience is to embrace it and turn the loss of exclusive identification with ego into the transforming sacrifice of coming into deeper relation to the Self. This is what I do. The dream is paradoxical: it's a "good" dream, a dream about a more intimate relation to the divine. But I experience it as a "bad" dream because it is frightening and overwhelming from the ego's point of view.

Though not all nightmares are representations of the struggle between the ego and the Self, they are representations of the struggle between the ego and the unconscious (whose purposes, from a Jungian perspective, are determined by the Self). The unconscious clamors for our attention, determined to give us the knowledge and experiences that we need to move towards wholeness and, ultimately, connection with the divine. Every gathering in of unconscious material strengthens the relationship between the ego and the unconscious, thus, ultimately, the ego and the Self. Frightening dreams about the divine seem to represent a kind of high noon of spiritual development, in which the ego as it is must die but will be reborn in another form.

Given the challenge of forming and reforming the ego-Self axis, it is not surprising that we are often profoundly ambivalent about our relation to the Self. The ego's point of view is much easier to live with. The kind of objectivity about one's self, realistic understanding of others' points of view and general clear-sightedness about one's place in the overall scheme of things works against the unexamined assumption that one is the center of the universe that is such a common feature of human life. In his book *The Road Less Traveled*, M. Scott Peck talks about the importance of having the qualities that come with a deeper connection with the Self, which enable us to sometimes be a therapist in our relationships with others, and the typical human ambivalence about living in this way:

> Occasionally when patients ask me when they will be ready to terminate their therapy, I will reply, "When you yourself are able to be a good therapist." This reply is often most usefully made in group therapy, where patients of course do practice psychotherapy on each other and where their failures to successfully assume the role of psychotherapist can be pointed out to them. Many patients do not like this reply, and some will actually say, "That's too much work. To do that means that I would have to think all the time in my relationships with people. I don't want to think that much. I don't want to work that hard. I just want to enjoy myself." Patients often respond similarly when I point out to them that all human interactions are opportunities either to learn or to teach (or to give or receive therapy), and when they neither learn nor teach in an interaction they are passing up an opportunity. Most people are quite correct when they say they do not want to achieve such a lofty goal or work so hard in life. The majority of patients... will terminate their therapy at some point far short of completely fulfilling their potential. They may have traveled a short or even a goodly distance along their journey of spiritual growth, but the whole journey is not for them.[2]

Our ambivalence is so profound that, even though we may be able to grasp intellectually that it is desirable to come to a deeper and different understanding than the ego's, we often don't want to do the work because it is seen as so difficult. The problem is, of course, that when we think about this consciously, we think about it from the ego's point of view, and from the ego's point of view, this shift of perspective is dangerous to the ego's illusory sovereignty.

This ambivalence also comes out in dreams. The familiar dream of trying to run but being able to move only slowly or not at all is a dream that, among other things, expresses this ambivalence.[3] We are partly spirit, but that spirit has its present home in a body with which the ego identifies, which is not as sprightly as spirit. We want to have a closer connection with the divine, but on the other hand we don't; it makes life much harder. Such dreams are reminiscent of Kierkegaard's description of the development of passionate inwardness, his way of describing the struggle in human beings to come into conscious relation with our condition as both existential and divine, and to make the leap of faith required for commitment to a relation with the divine:

> I have often thought about how one might bring a person into passion. So I have considered the possibility of getting him astride a horse and then frightening the horse into the wildest gallop, or even better, in order to draw out the passion properly, the possibility of getting a man who wants to go somewhere as quickly as possible (and therefore was already in something of a passion) astride a horse than can hardly walk—yet existing is like that if one is conscious of it. Or if a Pegasus and an old nag were hitched to a carriage for a driver not usually disposed to passion and he was told: Now drive—I think it would be successful. And this is what existing is like if one is to be conscious of it. Eternity is infinitely quick like that winged steed, temporality is an old nag, and the existing person is the driver, that is, if existing is not to be what people usually call existing, because then the existing person is no driver but a drunken peasant who lies in the wagon and sleeps and lets the horses shift for themselves. Of course, he also drives, he is also a driver, and likewise there perhaps are many who—also exist.[4]

Kierkegaard offers us a vivid picture of what it is to be a human being, capable of consciousness and relation to the divine, who also exists in time and space and must make choices in ways that do justice to both aspects of our being. The Kierkegaardian world is not a comfortable one; it is full of conflict, uncertainty, and ambivalence. His notion of the leap of faith offers an image of both what is necessary and what is profoundly difficult and frightening about committing ourselves to a relation to the divine that is not intellectually comprehensible or justifiable.

The next dream belongs to Jake, a clinical psychologist who has had great success as an educator, writer, and clinician. He has a Lutheran background, though he has not continued his connection with the Christian church in any form. At one time he wanted to be a minister, but came to feel that this was more from a desire to please others and gain prestige than from a genuine call. His spiritual life is to a great extent lived out through his life as a musician, a hobby that turned into a passion. Here is his dream.

Limitation

I'm facing a Christ figure who's in a long white robe. He has his arms outstretched, palms forward. At his left side is a young girl, about seven or eight, who is stretching up her right hand to touch his left hand. They cannot touch. She is weeping and is in need of comforting. He is weeping also with the knowledge of the impossibility of his being able to truly comfort her. I begin to feel my way into him and how it feels to see, to experience, others' pain and sorrow and be unable to remedy it. He would like to be able to reach down and touch her hand, but he knows that he cannot—cannot provide the comfort and assurance that she needs. The gap remains. The feeling in the dream is of need, yearning, compassion, sorrow, impotence, and some resignation. On waking, there is a sense of "Yes, that's the way it is."

The image has stayed with me as a kind of representation of Jesus that I can accept as consistent with my own experience of how it must feel to look out onto the pain in the world that cannot be assuaged. How it must feel to know and yet be unable to touch, to comfort, to heal everything. So the image is of compassion, sorrow, willing-but-unable to remedy, yearning (on both sides) but unable to contact, yet refusing to turn away from the knowledge of suffering.

Jake felt that this dream had influenced him deeply. It is an image of living out the divine through entering into the sorrows of others. This is a realistic representation of one important aspect of being a therapist. Being a therapist entails being willing to enter into the sorrows of others, and doing so makes us realize how much sorrow there is the world. Our clients suffer, and they also come from families in which there is a great deal of suffering. Being a therapist attunes one to the suffering in the world, to the knowledge that for many, life is filled with pain and disappointment and loss. And even when we are able to offer our help, those who come to us sometimes cannot truly absorb it. In these cases, all we have to offer is our conscious, attentive presence, which means that we must enter into their suffering.

This is a dream of the dark side of the development of the ego-Self axis. It is also a dream of willingness to suffer, itself a spiritual transformation of the will. M. Scott Peck argues that a great deal of neurotic difficulty is caused by an unwillingness to suffer:

> Fearing the pain involved, almost all of us, to a greater or lesser degree, attempt to avoid problems. We procrastinate hoping that they will go away. We ignore them, forget them, pretend they do not exist. We even take drugs to assist us in ignoring them, so that by deadening ourselves to the pain we can forget the problems that cause the pain. We

attempt to skirt around problems rather than meeting them head on. We attempt to get out of them rather than suffer through them.

This tendency to avoid problems and the emotional suffering inherent in them is the primary basis of all human mental illness. Since most of us have this tendency to a greater or lesser degree, most of us are mentally ill to a greater or lesser degree.... In the succinctly elegant words of Carl Jung, "Neurosis is always a substitute for legitimate suffering."[5]

I would be inclined to say that it is also caused by an inability to suffer and a fear of suffering as a result of a fragile ego structure. This seems clearly to be so in the case of children, whose fragile partially developed egos would be destroyed by too much suffering. Jung takes a similar position about unconscious complexes: they become unconscious because their contents are unbearable. In general, most of us try to avoid suffering. Whole philosophical theories, such as the Utilitarianism of Jeremy Bentham and John Stuart Mill, are based on the theory that it is our human nature to seek pleasure and avoid pain. Thus a willingness to suffer, especially a willingness to be conscious of the parts of life that cause suffering, to pay attention to the darkness and pain not only of one's own life but in that of others, is a spiritual task. Gerald May distinguishes between willingness and willfulness: "willingness implies a surrendering of one's self-separateness, and entering-into, an immersion in the deepest processes of life itself. It is a realization that one already is a part of some ultimate cosmic process and it is a commitment to participation in that process. In contrast, willfulness is the setting of oneself apart from the fundamental essence of life in an attempt to master, direct, control, or otherwise manipulate existence. More simply, willingness is saying yes to the mystery of being alive in each moment. Willfulness is saying no or perhaps more commonly, "Yes, but...."[6] It is much easier to be willing when we are engaging with the joyful, pleasurable aspects of the mystery of life. However, willingness is truly tested when we are faced with saying "yes" to the dark and painful aspects. This is an image of Jesus as the unsuccessful aspect of the suffering servant: even though the suffering servant may be willing to suffer and die to make transformation possible, this does not mean everyone will be transformed. The existence of the possibility does not guarantee the actuality. This aspect of the divine was meaningful to Jake because it matched his experience; he did not experience Jesus as strongly Other, but as a being he could "feel his way into." He recognized this sorrowing, frustrated Jesus because he echoed Jake's own experience. It is this aspect of the divine that was able to incarnate in Jake, a willingness to enter into the suffering of others whether or not there is any certainty of being able to help. This is one of the features of unconditional love: it does not require reciprocation or reward, it is simply there. It is one of the characteristics of the Christian God, who is described in the traditions as loving human beings without reserve whatever they may do.

As well as noting what is present here, it is useful to note what is absent. The dream offers us an image of the sorrowing Christ. It is the opposite of Christ the triumphant Redeemer. This is the human Christ, with his limitations emphasized. It is also an essentially tragic view of human life. It is not that Jesus is unwilling, nor is the little girl not trying, but somehow it just cannot be. This aspect of life, that things go wrong, that we cannot have what we want, that sometimes even having what we want is not as satisfying as we had thought since it does not always result in the cessation of desire, that there is pointless suffering which cannot be assuaged, is an aspect of human life that has been described variously by philosophers and theologians. Jean-Paul Sartre's famous remark in *Being and Nothingness*, "Nothingness lies coiled in the heart of being—like a worm,"[7] is a metaphysical description of this aspect of reality. Karl Jaspers's notion of boundary situations such as suffering and struggle is also an acknowledgment of the permanence and pervasiveness of the uncontrollable pain and difficulty in human life. From a moral standpoint, the existence of systems of moral principle is an indication that we are aware that all is not always well, and that we do not automatically do what is good or right. Both the Epicureans and Stoics recognized that a fundamental moral task is to learn to live somehow with the fact that life is difficult, dangerous, and disappointing. The Christian notion of original sin addresses this as well. For all our current distaste for the notion that human beings are inherently sinful, it is nevertheless true that human beings have been and continue to be capable of the most appalling acts, even when we try mightily to be better. The novelist and philosopher Iris Murdoch suggests that Freud's analysis of the psyche is actually a psychologized version of original sin;

> Modern psychology has provided us with what might be called a doctrine of original sin.... When I speak in this context of modern psychology I mean primarily the work of Freud.... One may say that what he presents us with is a realistic and detailed picture of the fallen man.... What seems to me, for these purposes, true and important in Freudian theory is as follows. Freud takes a thoroughly pessimistic view of human nature. He sees the psyche as an egocentric system of quasi-mechanical energy, largely determined by its own individual history, whose natural attachments are sexual, ambiguous, and hard for the subject to understand or control. Introspection reveals only the deep tissue of ambivalent motive, and fantasy is a stronger force than reason. Objectivity and unselfishness are not natural to human beings.[8]

Murdoch's novels are filled with descriptions of the consequences of this situation, particularly selfishness, ruthlessness, and the resulting human misery.

This is an aspect of human life that requires our attention as both human beings and therapists, and it is an aspect that calls out for a complex understanding of the divine, especially if we are also spiritual directors.

One of the dangerously seductive consequences of feeling a strong contact with the divine, and believing that the divine is healing, is the view that somehow every human ill is "fixable" by the divine. This view often entails that if one's ills are not "fixed," this is an indication of lack of faith or some other serious personal failing. That this is not the case is particularly clear to spiritual directors, who have constant contact with people who have deep faith, and a sense of the presence of the divine, and still suffer from life's misfortunes. For them, the possibility of healing of the soul may or may not be connected with the healing of the body or of adverse circumstances. The healing of the soul may consist in finding meaning in suffering, but this is not the same thing as ending suffering. It is a deeper way of living it out. That suffering is unavoidable and ineliminable is a significant insight that enables those participating on both sides of therapy/analysis and spiritual direction to face into the darkest aspects of life without trying to rationalize them in terms of what is acceptable to us.[9] In Jung's essay "Answer to Job," he argues that Job's power in the situation is his refusal to resign himself to what has happened to him, or to assume that his troubles are due to some explicable human failing of his, as his friends claim. He does not minimize his suffering, or try to explain it away. He feels strongly that he has been a good man, and that God owes him some kind of explanation. In the end, God presents him with the only possible explanation: God's ways are not our ways, and we must love and fear God anyway. Jung believed that Job's tenacity had an effect on God, or on the way God could be experienced, so that God became more respectful and compassionate, sending his only son to become human and suffer.[10] Looking at it a slightly different way, Job faced not the wrath of God, but the absolute Otherness of God. Part of our experience of the unavoidability of human suffering is our confrontation with a spiritual choice: we can believe there is no divine and no meaning, or we can believe there is a divine and some meaning which is not available to us. As we can see in Job, this is not an entirely arbitrary choice. Job's deep faith does not give him the option of not believing, which might in many ways be easier. One might just tough it out and wait for things to improve. Because Job's conviction of God's presence and God as ground of Being is so profound, he cannot choose that option. Because he can consciously hold the tension of great suffering and faith in God, Job has the opportunity to confront God, and in this confrontation, his identification with the ego's point of view is finally ended. Though many scholars have argued that the ending to Job is a later addition, it is also not out of place. It is the image of abundant life, returning with his new point of view. While Job seems to experience a classic if somewhat callous happy ending (his family is "replaced"), it is also true that those with a deep connection to the divine may experience a sense of abundant life while continuing to suffer from illness and misfortune.

Jake's dream raises an issue that is a constant in psychotherapy: not all suffering is redemptive. Redemptive suffering exists, in the sense that there is often a great deal of voluntary suffering in the death and rebirth of the ego that occurs when a strong connection is made with the Self, and important transformations can take place when we can come to view loss as sacrifice, as having a transformative meaning. This suffering, which occurs in both the dark night of the senses and the dark night of the soul[11] is often attenuated and even seems endless, yet finally is experienced as an essential part of the path to meaning. The fact that it is accepted and in that sense undergone voluntarily is an essential part of its redemptiveness. The suffering in Jake's dream is not the suffering that leads to an altered experience of meaning. Rather, it seems to represent both involuntary suffering and suffering connected with the knowledge that such suffering is often unassuageable and a constant in human life. This gives it a deeper meaning than simply Jake's regret and sadness about his own limitations. It portrays suffering itself as a divine activity when it is experienced in connection with our compassion for the suffering of others. Thus Jake's dream is a "bad" dream in that it does not seem to offer a way out of suffering. At the same time, it dignifies suffering by connecting it with the divine: not only does Jake suffer, but the divine in the form of Jesus also suffers over the human condition. This is one of Jake's experienced connections to the divine: he is willing to enter into the suffering of others with compassion, whether he can do anything about it or not. This willingness has a spiritual significance; from the standpoint of the comfort of the ego's point of view, Jake need not do this. As discussed above, many people resist entering into the suffering of others with great energy because their desire to avoid pain is so strong. The image of Jesus in the dream speaks strongly of suffering voluntarily embraced.

Both these dreamers seem to identify unconsciously with Jesus, suggesting an unconscious theological view. There is considerable variation in the Christian tradition in views about who Jesus is and what our relation to him ought to be. Both of these dreamers seem to believe that our task is to be Jesus rather than to worship him from afar. For both, their own images of struggle and suffering reflect Jesus's experiences. Interestingly, Jesus plays an important part in both my personal and corporate spiritual life and not in Jake's, and Jesus appears in Jake's dream but not in mine. The reference to the sleepers in the garden in my dream suggests an identification with Jesus's path, but he does not appear in person. One thinks here of Jung's view that dreams are compensatory, balancing the conscious attitude with more material from the unconscious.

"Bad" dreams about the divine can be as important as ones that we find inspiring and hope inducing. They keep us from slipping into fantasy about the joys and protective effects of spiritual life. They force us to face the basic human condition, which contact with the divine helps us to live out at a deeper, more conscious level, but will not cure. This is especially important in our culture, where advertising and media represent life as a soluble problem if we only have enough technology, attractive material things, and financial security.

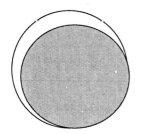

7

Tiffany's
Transformation

One of the greatest challenges in my work as both therapist and spiritual director has been working with people who are so deeply wounded they feel that their depths contain nothing but pain and suffering. Those who are the victims of abuse and other kinds of trauma at first experience work with the unconscious as increasing their suffering. As well, and understandably, many feel that there is no such thing as the divine, because if there were, they would have been rescued from their childhood suffering. If they do believe in God, they are angry with God, bitter at being abandoned to the brutality of those around them. In some instances, such as Heather's dream of the comforter and Jane's dream of God as the lover of her soul, the divine comes into consciousness through dreams that contain healing experiences. Since healing is what they most need, healing is the form in which the divine comes. However, while not everyone is able to have these kinds of experiences of the divine, psychically they require some indication of the divine's existence. I encounter more such clients in my private therapy practice than in my spiritual direction work, but I bring my concern with the life of the spirit, both the client's and mine, into all my work and not just spiritual direction.

The next dream belongs to a client who has suffered more deeply than nearly any client I have ever worked with. The story of her childhood is the story of virtually continuous neglect and brutal physical and sexual abuse by both parents. Her parents were both alcoholics and completely absorbed in their self-destructive lifestyle. Her mother was probably psychotic, and her father was deeply depressed. They neglected their children, and as a very small child, Tiffany was left to care for her even smaller brother.

Extraordinarily, Tiffany told me she knew from the beginning that there was something wrong with her parents. She did not have the sense of "that's the way things are" that so many abused children have. She was constantly on the lookout for resources outside her family. She had many "substitute mothers" in her neighborhood. She took herself to Sunday school on Sundays. She vowed that she would never be like her parents, that she would be as nearly the opposite as possible. Courageous and determined, kind and empathic, she escaped an abusive marriage to live as a single mother and to do a fine job of raising her two daughters. First as a nurse, then as a therapist, she entered the helping professions. When I first met her, she had reached the limit of the coping strategies she had developed as a young girl. She had had several experiences of breakdown, been hospitalized, and was often suicidal. She had not felt helped by the psychiatrists and therapists she had seen, and had come to me in a last attempt to find a way through her suffering to a more satisfying way of being.

As Tiffany told me her story, I sometimes felt overwhelmed by the darkness of her childhood. Her memories were fragmented and terrifying. She remembered someone trying to drown her in the bathtub, but couldn't see a face to go with the hands. She dreamed of blood and knives and butchered babies, of being chased by monsters and knowing that they would certainly catch her. She dreamed of violence and betrayal and frustration. These images pursued her into her waking life; she experienced repetitive imagery of her sexual abuse, and saw monsters waiting for her in the corners of her room when she tried to sleep. She was enraged, often suicidal, and drank to kill the pain, which only made her feel worse.

During the time we worked together, I found myself wanting to give her things to help her hang on. I gave her pictures of angels to put in her bedroom to help chase away the monsters. I lent her a Jerusalem cross to put under her pillow. I gave her a rosary. I felt all along that she had a connection to the spirit as well as a powerful life force. She often told me that she didn't believe in God, that she couldn't believe in a God that would allow a child to suffer the way she had. At the same time, I thought she found it comforting that I did believe. She used to tease me gently about it, and I felt that was her way of connecting with my belief.

We went through some very hard times together. During one of her worst periods, when she was deeply depressed and suicidal, I began to be afraid. I was afraid that she would attempt suicide and be successful at it— she had made at least one serious attempt before I knew her. I was afraid she might drive while drinking and hurt or kill herself and others. I felt that the work we were doing together was having no impact on her, and that perhaps she would not be able to survive the return of memory and feeling that deep work brings. During one of my own darkest times, I had the following dream.

Prayer for Tiffany

> I am in a large room at the top of a building, a loft. I am wearing some kind of robe or toga. Tiffany comes in, draped in a sheet. She is in anguish, and she is supported on each side by a woman. At first she sits down on a couch, and begins to bend and writhe in agony. Then I signal the women to bring her over to a long table so that she can lie down. She stretches out on the table. I stand beside her and raise my arms to heaven in a gesture of prayer and supplication. The whole dream takes place in silence.

I found this dream meaningful on a number of levels. First of all, the ritualistic feel of the dream reflected a sense I had that what I did in our work together had to come from the deepest possible place, because from a conscious perspective I often had no idea what to do. I sometimes found the sheer intensity of her suffering intimidating. I often prayed for guidance and for her while we were in my consulting room together. As well, it seemed to reflect a point of connection between us. In some way, I connected Tiffany's suffering with issues in my own life, especially with my mother, who had been in a great deal of emotional distress, and with myself in relation to her. Finally, the dream gave me the sense that we had joined together in a sacred task. The table seemed to be an altar, and she lay down on it like a sacrificial victim. Her willingness to do this suggested to me that underneath her apparent resistance, anger, and bewilderment, she had truly entered into the process. Her position on the altar seemed to me to reflect her deep suffering and victimization by her parents. As well, it reflected my sense of her own profound struggles and her willingness to be vulnerable to the process in which we were both engaged. It also reflected the sense I had that she would need to be willing to make an enormous sacrifice to be healed. She would need to sacrifice the complex coping mechanisms she had developed, her rigid exclusion of her own anger from conscious life (because she was so afraid of being like her parents), a picture of herself as having to be always good and never bad (as her parents were) that had sustained her through her childhood and youth, and her desperate attempts to control what emerged from the unconscious and frightened her greatly. In short, something was being sacrificed; her old self. The altar suggested the possibility of healing as well as sacrifice. On a more secular level, I also thought of the table as an operating table, which suggested to me the radical nature of the change that Tiffany was undergoing. It was surgery rather than recovery from the flu.

Reflecting on my gesture of raised hands, I felt that the dream offered an image of invoking help from the divine and the hope of getting it. We both seemed to be dressed for a religious ceremony, and there was no conversation throughout. My robe and her sheet suggested to me both a religious ceremony and a medical procedure, which seems an appropriate image for both therapy and healing. Finally, the spiritual atmosphere in the dream seemed to speak of the closeness of the divine, of archetypal energies. Remembering Lionel Corbett's view that archetypal energies enter through the most wounded place because that is where the barrier between conscious and unconscious is weakest, the dream represents the possibility of entry of archetypal energies into the psyche, both hers and mine—hers because of her own profound wounding, and mine because of my strong commitment to her, not just as a therapist but for some reasons that came from my own personal issues.

This dream helped sustain me in my work with Tiffany. I felt that it affirmed my own integrity in the work, and my faith in a source other than my ego. I have often noticed that in working with very difficult and challenging clients, there is the potential for inflation, a sense of my own heroic efforts and importance in doing such difficult work. I suspect this is a compensation for my own suffering in the work. However, what is necessary for such work is the kind of humility that allows one to work from the deepest possible place, so that energy that is not the ego's can come through. This is especially important with clients who have had to manage great suffering psychically. Their defensive systems are so complex, their rage and sorrow are so profound, that understanding and knowing what to do from the ego's standpoint is impossible. This kind of work depends more than others on inspiration, and on an incursion of energy from the divine. It is not uncommon for me to pray during sessions; one of the most important contributions training as a spiritual director has made to my work as a therapist is the strong sense that the divine is present in the therapeutic field. In Jungian work, one is waiting for the unconscious to manifest itself in the field. The field itself emerges as a process involving the unconscious of both client and therapist.[1] What emerges comes from both, and at best from the deepest in both so that the therapist can speak from her or his own deepest place to the client's deepest place. In the work of spiritual direction, one is waiting for the will of the divine to manifest itself. Though in the end there is a great deal of overlap between these points of view, the sense that the divine is present in the process also allows one to call on the divine for help. This is an active psychic process that can assist waiting for something to emerge, and I have found it supporting and sustaining.[2]

After ten years of work together, Tiffany began to heal. She began to trust herself and others. She was able to be angry without feeling guilty. She developed a sense of well-being. This was especially noteworthy because she had developed serious physical difficulties that caused her to experience a great deal of pain. Nevertheless, her love for life was finally able to flourish, and she was able to address the difficulties of life as ordinary rather than overwhelming. All along, we had talked about her relation to the divine. I had suggested on several occasions that she might enjoy attending the Unitarian Church, with its emphasis on ethics and values rather than transcendence. She had strong ethical views, and I thought she might enjoy the company of others—loneliness was an ongoing problem. Though she didn't absolutely reject this idea, nothing ever came of it. Though she had attended Sunday school completely on her own, her adult point of view was still that of suspicion of any notion that there might be a God that she could be in contact with. She knew I prayed for her and she appreciated it, but she was not able to pray for herself. However, towards the end of our work together, she had the following dream.

The Test

I am taking a series of exams to qualify as a therapist. It is the last day of the exams. I hear a voice telling me that the final question on the exam is also the most important question on the exam. The question is: Why do you believe in God? The voice tells me that the answer must be twenty-three pages long. I say, "But I don't believe in God."

On the face of it, this is a discouraging dream. Tiffany is being asked a crucial question and she doesn't know the answer. In fact, from her standpoint in the dream, the question is impossible to answer. Given her views, she has no resources from which to construct an answer. Since the question is the most important question on her qualifying exam, it sounds as if she may fail. This interpretation makes it a "bad" dream. It seems to be a God-denying dream, a dream that reasserts her nonbelief in God. However, if we think of the dream from the standpoint of the dynamics of the psyche, it looks very different. Something in Tiffany does believe, and is telling her that this is the most important issue. The dream represents a demand from the Self to the ego that the ego is apparently unable to satisfy. In a sense, the ego is always unable to satisfy this demand. It can never explain why it commits itself to a relationship with the divine, because there are no adequate reasons for doing so. The ego depends on the authority of the Self for this commitment. This absolute conflict between the ego and the Self is connected with a profound issue that is raised in work with people like Tiffany. Like Tiffany, we want to ask, "Why do the innocent suffer? What kind of God, especially a God who claims benevolence, could allow this to happen to a tiny child? Why can't we eliminate suffering from the world?" These are questions from the point of view of the ego. It is a merciful and benevolent question, nevertheless, it is limited by the ego's point of view. There are so many possible answers to this question, but none of them satisfactory. Anyone who has taken a first-year philosophy course has probably heard and criticized all the standard arguments. Suffering makes us stronger, improves our character, is a punishment, brings some good in its wake. For those of us who actually witness the consequences of the profound suffering of small children, none of these answers is adequate. In fact, if any of these answers satisfy us, we have failed to grasp the depth of suffering that results from severe childhood abuse. We can never answer this question. Tiffany couldn't answer it, yet the depth of her nature called to her to consider the possibility that she might be able to respond to it in some way. The dream presents a situation that necessitates the activities of the transcendent function, an apparent contradiction that cannot be resolved through reason either abstract or practical. The paradox lies in the conclusion: through the denial of belief, the possibility of belief is raised. When Tiffany and I talked about this dream, she laughed a little. She knew how I had hoped for her to be able to connect to the divine, and she realized the dream pointed in that direction even though she had always vehemently resisted it. It was then that I realized that she had in a sense fooled both me and herself all along. I said, "It's not that you don't believe in God, is it? You're just completely enraged at God for all the things that happened to you." She looked at me as if I'd finally solved a riddle both for herself and for me. Looking at me from under her eyelids, she said "maybe" in a dry but humorous way that meant yes. At was at this point she reminded me that when she was a child, she used to go to Sunday school by herself, while her parents were sleeping off their hangovers. She had told me this very early in our relationship and, at the time, I had failed to grasp its significance.

She was very puzzled by this dream. She knew it was important—it had a numinous feel. But the ego's point of view in the dream coincided so completely with her vehement denial of any belief in God that she couldn't sort out why she thought it was so important. It wasn't until we talked about it that she realized that the dream was presenting her with the actual psychic situation. Something in her, from which she mostly felt cut off, knew how important a connection with the divine was for her. It was "the most important question on the exam." This was emphasized by its being an exam for qualification as a therapist. Becoming a therapist had always been central to her sense of becoming her authentic self. She has told me a number of times that she feels more like herself when she's working with clients than at any other time. Thus the voice in the dream tells her that, from the point of view of what is most authentic in her, her belief in God is essential. In a sense, like the dark dream that I had while training as spiritual director, it's another head-on confrontation between the ego and the Self.

What do these dreams tell us about the activities of the divine in the psyche? They tell us that the divine is finely attuned to our individual needs. This means that the divine can work both for and against ego strength, depending on what is needed in the moment. Spiritual life is often described as ego loss or relativization of the ego. However, we also need ego strength. Ann Belford Ulanov, in her collection *The Functioning Transcendent*, often points out that development of the ego-Self axis results in strengthening of the ego; the ego is not rigid, but flexible. The ego is able to use the Self as a resource. One knows one doesn't need to do everything through the use of will and consciousness, but can depend on the Self for support, inspiration, and direction. The dreams of Heather and Jane in chapter four showed us the Self/divine at work in the psyches of two women who were in crisis and on the verge of falling into despair. In both instances, their capacities to deal with the world as well as their faith in God were enhanced by these dreams. In the two dreams in chapter six, Jake's dream about Jesus being unable to reach the child and mine about the terrible sound, which seem darker and counter to the ego's needs, the Self/divine is challenging the ego: it is challenging the ego's rigidity, its limited picture of the world, its denial of the reality of the divine. Both of these dreams leave us wondering about the outcome. We do not see the resolution that is characteristic of the completed activity of the transcendent function. Rather, there is recognition of the tension between the opposites, which occurs while holding both and not denying either, which can stimulate the activity of the transcendent function. Tiffany's dream is one of these: a dream of the transcendent function, or, from a spiritual standpoint, grace, in process. The opposites are clearly present: the most important question on the exam for the most important activity in Tiffany's life is a question that presupposes a faith she does not have and indeed denies she has. Does the questioner know something she doesn't? Is this the self's way of approaching her, through the work she loves? She denies her belief, but her main feeling in the dream was surprise. To pass the exam, she must address the question to which she currently has no answer. This is the transecendent function at work.

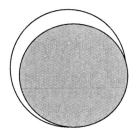

8

Grace's Grace-Filled Journey

This is the story of a long-term client, an extraordinary woman with extraordinary dreams and experiences. When she gave me permission to write about her life, she asked if I would call her Grace. It seemed entirely appropriate.

This case presentation is from my private practice rather than my practice in spiritual direction, and I have chosen it because it provides an excellent illustration of the psychological development that leads towards spiritual life, and of the appearance of specifically spiritual material in dreams.

Grace first came to me a number of years ago. A writer, she had recently moved to Vancouver. She was in a relatively new and difficult relationship, her mother had recently died, she did not know many people in Vancouver, and she was in great distress: anxious, sad, and depressed. She had mixed feelings about the death of her mother, who had been a depressed, narcissistic, and demanding parent. Grace felt both relief and grief, as well as lost. Her father had died several years before. When she first began to see me, Grace was forty-three. She had lived in both Canada and the United States and considers herself both Canadian and American. Her religious background is Unitarian, which is somewhat unusual in Canada.

There are themes in Grace's life; the first and most important one has to do with boundaries. Grace's mother had very poor boundaries; she had difficulty distinguishing between Grace and herself, and Grace was expected to mother her mother. Her parents had separated and her father had abandoned the family, leaving them in extreme financial difficulty. Soon after this abandonment, Grace's only sister, who was older than Grace, left as well. This left

Grace with her mother, who was often so depressed she was unable to get out of bed; she was also verbally abusive. Grace had the sense she was keeping her mother alive; her mother talked a great deal about "being at the end of her rope," of "not being able to go on," hence the threat of suicide was in the air. Grace's mother was jealous and envious of her youth, her intelligence, and her artistic ability. Though she did very well at school, Grace did not receive praise at home. Nothing she could do, and she did quite a lot, was ever good enough for her mother, who was endlessly critical and rejecting, saying things like "You don't know what love is" when she was displeased with Grace. When Grace saw her father, he too was demanding, critical, and cold. Cruel and sadistic towards his children when he lived at home, his coldness towards Grace and her mother after the separation was so extreme that he left them penniless. Grace had to go to him and beg for money for food. The result of all this for Grace was a diminished sense of self and entitlement and a history of people taking advantage of her with her permission. She was endlessly helpful, offering her considerable skill as a writer to others as an editor and sounding board while not taking time to do her own work. She had many friends who would call and talk for hours, unloading their troubles on her without giving her anything emotionally in return. Her relationship with her partner was difficult and she had trouble asserting her need for autonomy and privacy. She was very unhappy about all this, but had only recently become sufficiently aware of it to try and stop it.

Another related theme was Grace's bad judgment about people. Desperate for love, Grace allowed herself to trust the untrustworthy and had been hurt over and over again both personally and professionally. She had not been able to develop much discernment around who cared about her and who didn't, or who would respect her work and who wouldn't, so she had been unable to protect herself.

My portrait will not be representative unless I add that there is something quite special about Grace. She has a kind of glow, an aura of intelligence, wit, and spirit that is unusual. One can feel the presence of a very individual sensibility. I suspect this is one reason Grace's mother "chose" Grace rather than her sister as her support. As Alice Miller describes such situations in *The Drama of the Gifted Child*, her mother wanted to appropriate Grace's intuitiveness and vital spirit, and, for a time, she did.

This is Grace's presenting dream.

Big Baker

> For the first time I dream that I am other than myself, and not at all surprised to be a six-foot-six woman in a juicy, round figure and face, with an untamed flop of golden hair—round and soft and full of life. And a baker of bread in what feels like an olden

time, but the only world I see is my huge kitchen of wood and brick, with stove fires roaring warmly. A crew of six small scrawny bakers, men and women, and all whiny, with pinched faces, come to me with the general complaint—they have in their hands small shrivels of unused and unusable dough. It's waste that costs them that the small bakers can't do anything about. And I tell them, "It's good for something." Then I take all the scrap dough in my hands, rolling it all into one. The dough not only makes a loaf, but one large golden loaf baked right in my hands. And so I say, "It's for life."

This dream contains many of Grace's issues, both dark and light. It contains her aspiration to fully inhabit the feminine, her need to be her own mother, her need for life. It shows that even though she feels consciously depressed and unable to care for herself in the way she'd like, she has immense inner resources that can help the poor little whiny skinny parts. She knows how to solve the problem of wasted dough, she knows how to make a big nourishing loaf out of scraps. Grace has dreamed of herself as the Divine Mother. What is especially interesting about this dream is the intensity of the contrast between Grace's conscious attitude and her identification with the Divine Mother in the dream. She is large, she is creative, she is resourceful, and at the same time, she is not inflated. Grace's dream is not of archetypal identification, but of being able to embody the archetype while at the same time being able to maintain contact with her ego self.

Later in the same month, Grace had the following dream.

Gelatinous Murk

I wake up feeling the presence of something and see at the end of my bed, to the left-hand side, a large grim cloud hovering above the floor. Oozing greyness, this gelatinous murk ripples as it hovers, the undulations showing different light and colors, not reflected from without but from within, revealing colors and parts of my mother, who died almost a year ago—her hair, her skin, a turquoise dress I made for her. I am sick with terror and don't move. Suddenly I hear a deep male voice calling my name into my right ear, and I wake up.

This vivid image of her mother's unhappiness and her enveloping qualities evoke a sense of impending spiritual death: Grace is terrified. Perhaps the murk is what it felt like to be around her mother–bits and pieces of a human being embedded in a dark, threatening goo. Perhaps it is an image of Grace's inner mother, not nourishing but terrifying and potentially overwhelming. An interesting detail of this dream is the left-right symbolism: the murk is on

Grace's left hand, while the deep masculine voice that calls her name and calls her into consciousness is in her right ear. As we shall see, the divine is represented most often as a masculine figure in Grace's dreams. One thinks too of Sartre's concept, much (and rightly) criticized by feminists, of slime as feminine, as being in itself rather than being for itself, opposed to consciousness and even dangerous to it.[1]

Two months later, Grace had the following dream.

The Burned Man

> I am at the window of my house, but it doesn't feel like home: I live here, but it belongs to someone else and I am only someone passing through town. But there is a pleasure to being here, one that connects me to this place, that I get from watching a shop at the corner. There's a nice man who works there, who owns the place: an ordinary man with great kindness. He watches out over the neighborhood, making sure everyone is okay and giving the poor kids candy, and I watch him watch.
>
> But I also see the kids, hiding behind the shop, making fun of him, and suddenly his shop is burning down. The kids he gave candy to have set his shop on fire. In the wreck there are people hurt and burned beyond recognition. But I know which one the man is. Even though he can't speak and his body is burned over with a black crust, I can feel him alive inside; I can feel the force of his emotions. Those same ones pound inside my chest. By placing my hand above his chest I feel that he has love in him, and a great heart; that is how I know it's the shopkeeper. By heart.
>
> Everyone cares for the shopkeeper, but it seems there's nothing to do, and there's nothing he can do; he can't even wear clothes to protect himself. So he lies naked in a bed draped with gauze. I come and see him, to talk to him and be with him. There's more I want to give him but it seems there's nothing he, being so badly burned, can receive. And so I pluck from my dress, from my chest, a pearl button and I lay it on his chest. It seems that it's all I have to give, and it's so little. But on him, on the burned man's chest, the pearl button melts. I am so worried that I've only hurt him more, I want to take the button back, but the button has grown. It now stripes his body with mother of pearl, and his burned flesh turns into stripes of ebony, entirely covering his body. And it is his body: he's no longer human but a human work of art. And protected and beautiful. And so I watch, thrilled with wonder, as he rises and begins to move and live.

This dream seems to represent Grace's adjustment to life as a "nice" person, giving out candy to apparently grateful children who turn out not to be so grateful after all. The children are angry, spiteful, and destructive, much like Grace's experience of the friends to whom she gave her time and support, and by whom she was badly treated. It also seems to have to do with Grace's rage, her furious child who wants to burn that nice person who doesn't see to it that her real needs are fulfilled but rather gives her candy. This rage is expressed in the children's tormenting behavior. Finally it also expresses her powers for transformation, the power of her giving him a small but significant pearl, which seems to have both the qualities of the widow's mite and the pearl of great price.[2] Both of these are images of love and/or soul, and when Grace gives him soul, when she makes this compassionate connection with him, he is not only healed but also transformed. Grace was very interested in the image of the pearl, and I suggested to her that she get a pearl for herself. The next time I saw her, she had found a lovely pearl brooch that spoke to her sense of the dream, and she continues to wear it with pleasure.

Three months later, Grace had the following dream, which she experienced as deeply significant and transforming.

The Living Lake

On a warm summer evening I am walking up north in the wilderness with a beautiful young man who has black curly hair and brown eyes like melting chocolate. He is strapping, buoyant, spirited, and loving. He feels like he is my new love, my mate. The place becomes familiar, and I know I am near the lake where my family cottage used to be. But instead of taking the road, I want to take a new way, through the wilds. And my young man is game. We follow the sound of rushing water and come to small swirling rapids, and I know the lake is on the other side. I can see it and the encircling trees are richer and greener than I ever knew them, and the lake a deep blue.

With my young man on my right I suddenly feel the presence of a woman on my left. The Lady of the Lake, she beams at us with her large, luminous green eyes. She wears nothing but long curling red hair, and stands tall and broad and round in the lake. She is a part of it, as if it were her skirt. Right away I know she is a magic being, and without saying a word, my young man knows, too. The feeling of her presence is like being near solid strength. In her hands she holds a fish, a black cooked salmon with shimmering red and blue colors on it. The Lady of the Lake in her rich voice tells us, "This is the lake of life." She dips the salmon into it, and as the water touches it, the fish turns silver and shimmery—uncooked—comes back to life and swims away. I turn and look at my young man and in his eyes I see nothing but love. And so I take off my clothes and wade deep into the water of the lake of life, feeling the warm sandy bottom on my feet, and cooling waters.

When I walk out on the shore, I look down and notice my belly is large and hanging low; I'm pregnant from a walk in the water. And so I wade back into the lake, feeling that this magic comes and goes, and touch of water will undo this pregnancy. But when I come out, I am massively, hugely pregnant. The Lady of the Lake takes one look at my belly and says "It's a girl." I touch my belly and feel how solid and firm I am with a baby girl inside me. There's something of a trick going on here, and my own foolishness, I feel. And so I look at my young man and he beams back at me with the joy of love. And we say without words, as if our thoughts speak aloud, "A girl that comes from this magic is one to keep." As soon as I hear the thought I know it's true.

This dream marked a turning point for Grace. There is a sense of returning home, "through the wilds," the unconscious, joined with a beautiful and developed masculine figure. Perhaps the most powerful part of the dream is the appearance of the Lady of the Lake, a divinely powerful maternal image whose skirt is the lake of life, life so powerful that it has the power to bring a cooked and blackened salmon back to life, and to impregnate Grace just through her being in it. This is a highly feminine version of divine conception, making it clear that it is not only the patriarchal God who has the power to bring about the birth of the soul. The Lady of the Lake is reminiscent of the Big Baker in Grace's presentation dream,[3] and the blackened fish of the burned shopkeeper in the Burned Man dream, before his transformation into a living being in pearl and ebony. There is imagery here of both birth and rebirth. The rebirth of what has been burned and the birth of a divine child through being immersed in magical water give this dream a strong alchemical feel.

Grace experienced this dream as powerful and numinous. She literally felt different when she woke up than she did upon going to sleep. She felt that she had more life, that something had lifted. In the dream she plunges into the waters of life, with all the associations of baptism, the alchemical bath, and thriving organic life. She experiences the divine marriage and her pregnancy with her own soul. Grace's first powerful dream experience with the divine was with a golden figure, who appeared in a dream she had as a child. Her need for the feminine divine is clear from her presentation dream, as well as from her clearly inadequate mothering and indeed suffering at the hands of her mother. Notice that both the Big Baker and the Lady of the Lake are large women. Large women represent for her an abundance of life and energy and, finally, her own capacity to become pregnant with herself.

Like Joseph to Mary, her young man is with her in a loving way, but the conception takes place without him, and before the final loving gaze that solemnizes their union. Synchronously, Grace's reality reflected the images from her unconscious. Grace had recently told me that when she imagined her ideal therapist, before she ever came to see me, she imagined a large woman with a round face, dark hair in a bun, an American with intellectual interests. She told me that when I first opened the door to her, she "recognized" me. Grace needed a substantial feminine presence in real life as a support and as a "way in" to her relation to the divine, and she got one. I say "got" rather than "found" because she had a strong sense of something having been given to her without having had to search exhaustingly and exhaustively.

Four months later, Grace started having another kind of dream about her relation with the divine, one that introduces the masculine divine.

Golden Boys in the Basement

It's late and I am still working, doing a kind of quality control, checking over lyrics, making sure there is some kind of meaning or substance in an important piece of pop music for a record company in a fancy glass building. Yet again I'm working late, wearing a plain golden dress, alone, tired, and driven. Then suddenly I hear the sound of others in a building where no one else should be. And I follow the noises, without any fear, but an aching curiosity drawing me on. The sounds take me to the back of the new glass building, and I find it was built onto an old factory from the turn of the century.

Down the stairs I follow the noise, and the lower I go the older the building is, like something out of Dickens, and then with medieval brick and stonework. Finally, at the bottom of the stair well I come out into an old Roman underground aqueduct, glowing from a golden light. And I know it must be a magic place. There are three young teenage boys working here, collecting old classical music—Bach, Brahms, Mozart, Mahler—these boys have all of it, the most gorgeous music there has ever been. And the boys, too, are magical: golden skinned with golden eyes. One of them, with shiny brown hair and dark eyes looks at me like a shy boy feeling beaming love. And I see that they are all looking at me like that—they have always loved me, and have unearthed this music for me. And as they uncovered it below I knew it above and used it to turn into pop music. Never was I doing "quality control," as I thought.

I feel so badly that they cared for me all along, working harder for me than I did, and I never knew. So I take all their records in a wooden box, and sadly, nearly grieving as I go,

leaving them behind, I carry all their music up with me so the
golden boys don't have to work any more for me.

This dream, with its images of the divine masculine working in the deep
unconscious, generating creativity that is turned into trivial "pop music," made
Grace feel very sad. It made her even sadder to think that she had to lose
touch with them. She interpreted her taking the records away as her feeling
that she had to do everything through consciousness and will, thus depriving
herself of the contact with the deeper levels that she longed for. In light of this
dream, she resolved to have more respect for her own creativity and its life,
which she had given away to others in such quantity, used for trivial purposes
and not honored and taken possession of as she had wanted to.

This dream is especially interesting for its introduction of golden boys
from the classical period as the deepest level. These magical boys come from a
pre-Christian time, when the connection between the aesthetic and the religious was as important as the connection between the moral and the religious, and not viewed with the suspicion that characterizes a substantial aspect
of the Christian attitude towards the pleasurable rather than didactic aspect of
art. Grace connects the creative and the divine. This is a dream that specifically emphasizes her relation to her work and to creative life, and a dream in
which magical teenaged boys play exactly the same part that an anima figure
would play in the dream of a man. I have long suspected that the animus can
be a creative resource for women, as the anima is for men. For men, the
anima is often a guide, leading a man into his unconscious and introducing
him to his creativity or deepening his relation to it. In Grace's dream, she is
lured into the depths by the sounds of the golden boys' activities and finds
them working on her behalf. Unlike many anima dreams, these young men
are not elusive or seductive but loving and reassuring: they have always loved
her, always been there for her. Interestingly, one of the first dreams Grace
vividly remembers from childhood is about a golden boy; they really have
always been there for her. It's also interesting that Grace is now wearing a
plain golden dress. She seems to have incorporated some of the golden feminine that characterized the Big Baker in her presentation dream as she moves
into relation with the masculine.

Like the others, this dream is meaningful on three levels. On the existential level, Grace had to use her creativity to survive in her difficult life rather
than for its own sake, yet it continued to serve her. This dream also reflects
Grace's sense of always having had to work very hard (she had worked since
she was fifteen), being able to be expansive in a sense (an important piece of
pop music in a fancy glass building) but engaged in "quality control" on
things that were not of great intrinsic importance, such as editing the work of
others. On the inner level, it reflects Grace's having had to identify strongly

with her ego, using effort and will to live, and being able to reconnect with deeper sources only to feel she could not stay with them; she still has to keep working and trying, using what could be profound and meaningful (Bach, Mahler) to turn into pop music—whatever she needed just to get along. Finally, the dream contains the image of the young masculine divine—and quite a lot of it, continuing to work for her even as she consciously disconnects from it—and locates a part of Grace's spiritual sensibility in the classical, pre-Christian world.

One month later, she had the following dream.

Aristotle Visits

I am working late, alone, in the kitchen on a project, trying to figure out how to defend and protect ideas I'm developing. Suddenly at the doorway that leads into the hall I see an old man with flashing blue eyes, wearing a toga. I know him from a dream I had years ago, and love him, feeling in his presence that his wisdom transfers to me. I pull back the curtain to have a closer look at the wise old man, and as I look at him I can hear him speak without any words—a warning that someone is coming to the door. Right then, the aging owner of the building is at the apartment door having been wandering the building, lost, looking disheveled, and thinking this is his apartment—and wanting to come in. Normally I would be nice and let the fellow in, but I know I have to get him out. I say, "It's not your home," and close the door. Without looking at the wise old man, I can see him and this is right, and right away I wake up.

Grace experienced this dream as numinous, and it worked for her on every level. On the existential level, it specifically mentions her work, which is no longer on pop music but on her own ideas. She is trying to discover how to protect and defend them, how to hold her boundaries. The wise old man's presence allows her to do this, to throw out the disheveled building owner rather letting him in out of "niceness." I suspect the building owner is also an image of Grace's father, who only valued her for her physical attractiveness and "femininity" and not for her true self.

At the inner level, this dream presents Grace in her ego self having incorporated herself as a creative person discovering her relation to the Wise Old Man and the way in which he can help her to be discerning about what she includes and what she leaves out. She doesn't have to just let anything that knocks come in. It also introduces the idea that she is capable of wisdom, that she has her own resources to call on. Grace later identified the Wise Old Man as Aristotle; this indicates Grace's growing conscious respect for her own mind. Grace is an extremely intelligent and witty woman with considerable education, but she has tended to underestimate and underrepresent this aspect of herself.

From the standpoint of her relation to the divine, this is another masculine figure from the classical period. She felt strongly she wanted to come into stronger relation with him, and I suggested she make a drawing of him and use it like an icon in a simple meditative practice, which she did. Upon later reflection, she identified him as Aristotle and began to read Aristotle. She found his work on aesthetics resonant and meaningful, and continues to read him.

Partly as a result of her increased contact with the divine and the increased ego strength it gave her, Grace began to confront her rage.

Young Rage

I'm going to the corner store in the late evening, having worked too late, and I'm angry at my work partner for ruining the work, which I had to redo. I enjoy the view of the store as I stand in the parking lot looking through the window at the abundance within the shop. It makes me want to act and so I go to the phone booth and start to call my working partner to tell him how angry I am, and sort this out. I look over my shoulder to make sure I'm safe. There is someone there watching me, a young man, tall with a broad chest, waiting in the shadows. I realize he's me and I stand there, stunned, shocked, and frightened.

He starts coming for me, zooming not walking. And I see he wasn't in the shadows at all—he himself is made of the darkness. He stands right before me, an inch away, this black figure of youth. I feel him touch me, although he hasn't. I feel the smoothness of his T-shirt, the tightness of his stomach muscles, and the rage inside his belly, and how young he is. I feel this because his rage is now also inside my belly.

And I stand my ground. I know I could swing a good right hook at him. But he knows this too. As soon as I show no fear, he backs away. Now he stands under the light in the parking lot, but he is still only darkness. Then he steps out and vanishes as a shadow in the night.

Calmer now, I decide not to call my work partner, because I'm ready to talk face to face, and ready to bring changes to the work, not merely fix what was there before.

In this dream, Grace confronts her anger head on. This is important for her, since being "good" has been one of the burdens of her life. She is afraid of the power of her anger and experiences its strength. Doing this is transformative for her; she is ready to face her work partner with a new approach. In this dream, Grace experiences the complexity and resilience of her own being. She begins with fear, goes on to perception and courage, and finally reaches a kind of resolution, which seems to occur as a result of her choosing to be conscious and stand her ground.

Four months later, Grace entered into a struggle with evil.

Four Evil Men

I step outside my apartment building to enjoy the early fall evening, the sunset, the children rushing up the hill, so innocent. Suddenly I see a man across the street who's tall, solid, plain, and dressed in a trench coat and boots. He's hiding in the bushes, watching the children. Instinctively, I know this is not good. I look down the road and I see another man who looks just like the first, and this one is hiding by a tree, watching the children. Now I know I must look up the road, and there I see yet another man, nearly identical, beside a car. He's also watching the children and waiting. And now I know there is one in each direction, and so there's one near me. I don't have to look anymore, for I can feel him by my building.

Something's wrong and something's going to happen to the children. I am the only adult and I have to do something. But I don't know what. I simply turn to the man near my building and talk to him normally, about the lovely evening. Then I go across the road to the man hiding in the bushes, and the first man follows. I speak about the weather to the man in the bushes. Then I go downhill, to the man by the tree, and speak to him. Now I go up the hill to the man by the car and chat to him. And they have all followed me. The children keep on rushing by, going home, noticing nothing, but laughing—and innocent.

Now I have the four men together, I can see their faces are bland, numb, and neutral: don't seem human, they hardly seem alive to this life. I know they're a kind of evil. And I now see that, where they were wearing a boot, they all have a horn growing out of their right feet. Now that I see what they are I know what I am to do. I raise my right foot and stomp down on one of the horns. I think it's going to hurt—the horn might tear right through my own foot—but when I bring my foot down, the horn crumbles like an eggshell. Then I stomp all the horns down. When I am done I wake up with joy.

Grace felt that she had lost her innocence at a very young age. She had been utterly unable to defend herself against her father's contempt and criticism when he was present, and then was devastated by his abandonment. His cruelty and emotional sadism felt evil to her. She was left by him to care for her mother emotionally in order to have one even minimally functioning parent. The men in Grace's dream are dangerous, even demonic. She wants to save the children, and, as in the dream about her anger, her willingness to confront and even be aggressive with what she sees as dangerous and wrong for the children is successful. She is able to disarm the demons and save the children without injuring herself. Notice her willingness to sacrifice herself: she thinks it will hurt, but she must do it anyway. This willingness to sacrifice herself turns a situation of potential loss into a victory for the good. The children's innocence is saved and she is unharmed and wakes up filled with joy. She has saved herself from evil as lifelessness, and brought more "child" energy into her life unharmed.

One month later, she had the following dream.

God Comes to Dinner

I walk down a food aisle at my local grocery store, buying provisions. Behind me I notice a beautiful man, who's tall, broad, and burly, dressed in a workman-like checked shirt, pants, and boots, but he has golden hair and golden eyes. And his skin, too, gleams golden—not painted like a gold statue, but because his blood is gold. I am struck by the great yet simple male beauty he is.

I pick up a large carton of milk, and he smiles bashfully— yes. Then I pick up a large piece of fine cheese, and the golden man nods—yes. And I get bread and oysters, sweets and caviar, for our supper, all the while feeling very moved by his presence.

At home in the kitchen we make dinner. And as we're about to eat, he sits down, and for the first time I see how large he is. He's massive. I am to him as a child. He takes me into his arms and sits me on his lap. He draws a finger across each of my eyelids and says in a deep and sweet voice, "Let me take the clouds away." I feel so loved, as if my heart will break into a whole new heart, and think to myself, "Thanks God, I always wanted love like this."

Grace's golden boys and old man have now become a handsome young golden man, a man who can give her the love she needs. It seems clear that this is, for Grace, a relationship with the divine. This is her own sense of her dream, and the imagery is the kind of imagery that appears in the writings of the Christian mystics: the heart that breaks into a new heart, the love that finally satisfies. Many people who have been unloved and neglected as children feel that if only they could have enough love from another person, they would be healed. This is not the case; there is not enough human love in the world to fill that deficit in a wounded adult. The only love that suffices is divine love, which is infinite and healing. Grace's version of the divine is appropriate to her: she focused on God's earthly qualities. Her God loves milk, cheese, caviar, oysters. He is a God of sensual pleasure and bounty, the kind of God she needs after her emotionally deprived childhood, abandoned by a father who didn't even care whether there was enough food in the house. Notice too the correspondence between this image of God and Grace's feminine image of God in the "The Big Baker." Both are large, solid, strong—reassuring for the child of two cold narcissistic parents. Again, Lionel Corbett's observation comes to mind: the divine enters through the wounded places in the psyche.

After this, Grace had several dreams that seemed to focus on strengthening her sense of self, not having to perform for others, and taking her own desires, especially her desire for creativity, seriously. These dreams appeared over a space of about two months. Then, four months later, she had the following dream.

The Golden Blue Man

I am in the place which is my work studio. It's a lovely white room that is three steps down off of a large Spanish-style home. On three sides are windows—walls of windows looking out onto a green world. In one corner of the room is a grand piano, in another an easel, another is an empty corner—for thinking—and I am in the last corner. I am dressed tweedy, with a jacket and glasses, looking very much the grand dame novelist. I am at a small wooden desk, writing a book by hand.

In the middle of the room is a statue I made. It is a large deep-violet-blue man. A succulent man, round and jolly with a Buddha belly, and with a long, thick tapering tail. It's slung over one arm like a toga's train. The other arm is extended toward whoever walks down the stairs. I stare at him and walk around. He's wonderful, aesthetically, yet I thought I did more than that. I thought there was more life, more magic.

I turn away to brood on my lack of ability. And when I look back the statue has turned and looked at me. He's moved. I'm not sure of this, but as I step up closer I can see that his neck, his eyes, and parts of him that moved have turned to gold. I burst with joy. I *did* do more.

And then a friend comes to visit. She's dressed in black and there is a general grief about her—for her own life. She's come to see the statue and she admires it genuinely, saying, "It's very beautiful." I tell her that it's alive and say: "If you look at him long enough, he looks at you. There's gold everywhere he's moved." And as she looks at the statue, I look at her. But she turns to me and says: "I don't see it, don't see the gold. But I believe you, because I feel it." I thank her and I also feel some failure. I need to work on this statue more. And I also feel compassion for her,

for her loss of hope. It's clearer to me now—she thinks she'll
never have love.

This was a very important dream for Grace. Though at the time she was
working in film and television, she also wrote and continues to write short
stories and novels, and she feels this is her true calling. The dream affirmed
her in that feeling. The tweedy novelist felt like her authentic self. She also
makes contact with the part of herself that has been grieving over her difficult
and painful life, and cannot yet sense the presence of the divine that Grace has
created in the dream. This dream seems to present both hope and sorrow.
There is a part of Grace that is still sorrowful, that cannot see the gold. But at
the same time, what Grace has already done has given that part hope. Grace
has created something that has connected with the life of the divine, that is
not just a product of the ego. Grace has made the blue man, but he turns to
gold spontaneously as he moves and looks at her. He is her creation, and also
has life of his own. She sees him and he sees her. He seems to be an image of
the divine, both transcendent and animal, and also has a jolly Buddha belly,
another substantial image of the divine like the Big Baker and the Golden
Man who comes to dinner.

Grace worked with me for several years. She continued to develop,
through her own inner work and her flourishing dream life, images of the
divine that spoke to her. I would like to end Grace's story by saying that, first
of all, she has flourished in her life in the world. She is now happily married.
She has a child. She is working on a book that has been highly praised by
those who have seen the manuscript. Perhaps most importantly, she belongs
to herself. Interestingly, her spiritual life, so unusual and varied in her dreams,
is lived out in her waking life in relation to the Christian church. This is an
illustration of the fact that commitment to a spiritual path that involves a particular religious tradition by no means cripples creativity. It can do so in contexts that are limiting in that they exclude any imagery other than that
characteristic of their tradition, but many spiritual traditions, including some
traditions within the Christian church, do not do so. And Grace continues to
dream. This next dream, one of the last she had while we were working
together, brings us almost to the end of her story.

The Dream of Therapy with God

I am alone and looking for help, where I don't know, and
help doing what, I have no idea. So I stop myself and look
around, then I find myself in a place that no longer makes me
feel alone. It's not a kind of hiding place, but I am within a vast
expanse of blue, like being inside the sky.

I sit myself down in a chair, a simple kind of office chair, and then I begin to speak as if I'm in therapy. Yet, I don't find myself speaking about what sorrows or joys met me this week. I ask a primal and burning question: I can no longer write what I need to, but find myself in between the old way and a new one that does not exist, not even as an idea or a longing. That's not even known. I say how I want to write something of meaning, something of substance. I want to write life itself so that the reader experiences the work, the working, as alive—as an experience with the power and immediacy of their own existence.

Just then, I notice a fish, that is bright orange like an overgrown goldfish, and it's flying by my right side, near my head. Usually, I am completely terrified of fish, but not now. Because the fish is flying. It's not actually flying but swimming, because this endless gorgeous blueness that I'm within is the ocean. I'm at the bottom of the ocean, breathing water as if it is air—and feels like it, too. Any fear I have about the fish passes, even my astonishment at the lack of terror, because I'm sharing the fish's world.

That's when I notice I'm not talking in a therapeutic situation, yet soul searching, speaking aloud to myself alone. I sense a presence before me, sitting and listening. It is a presence that makes me feel more and more alive to be near it. And now I am aware of the feeling of this presence, of a being who is on the brink of appearing, and it is a buzzing and blurry phantom manifestation of an old man who is vital, who has a powerful and endless wisdom. He has a wild bush of white and grey hair, and a beard and the story I'm looking for. God has found it for me, and with me.

The imagery of this dream strongly suggested to Grace and to me a descent into the deep unconscious, the bottom of the ocean. She is in a different element, but she is at home there. Even though she is underwater, she can breathe. She has an important question and her way of dealing with it is very much the way a person of faith would enter into prayer. She sits down in a chair and begins to pour out her heart, even though apparently there is no one there. Gradually, a presence begins to materialize, a presence that is numinous and complex. The God who emerges has many features. From a Jungian standpoint, this is clearly a manifestation of the Self. From a Christian standpoint, this God seems to be related to the God of the Old Testament. But Grace describes him as a combination of Greek philosopher, Old Testament God, and Freud, Jung, and Blake's image of God. Though Grace's dreams of the divine have included golden young men from classical Greece and Aristotle, this God seems to represent an amalgamation of her various conceptions of spiritual life: philosophy, creativity, religious life, and therapy. She characterizes her relationship with this being as therapeutic: she is having therapy with God. And when she awoke, she felt different and has continued to feel different: more confident, more deeply in touch with herself. It is interesting to note that this is very much the conception of prayer that Ann Belford Ulanov offers in *Primary Speech*: "Desire leads each of us to begin praying from the premise of being, of who we are.... Surprises happen. We may discover we want more than we thought we dared. In the secret space of prayer, we may reveal to ourselves how much we want truth, beauty, love. In daily life, we usually hide from such desires, trying to protect ourselves from their urgency with cynical argument that those are merely childish hopes that life correctly disillusions. We may discover desire we did not know about or knew only dimly, desires that if followed would take us far off the path we have so carefully constructed."[4]

Grace's prayer is a prayer for creativity, for growth and authenticity in creativity. Grace's Unitarian background did not emphasize prayer, and I suspect this is one reason it is described as therapy. As well, therapy has become very meaningful to her. She has experienced it as a spiritual journey. She came into therapy deeply wounded, angry, and alienated. Largely through her work with dreams, she has discovered healing in her own depths and contact with the divine.

The shadow side of this dream lies in its subject matter and beauty. In order to survive her childhood with a highly narcissistic and intermittently suicidal mother, Grace developed the capacity to split off considerable portions of herself. Through our work, she has had wonderful dreams of divine energy, which she has struggled to bring into her everyday life of work and relationship. The images of this dream reflect not only the positive capacity to contact the divine at the deepest levels of the unconscious, but perhaps also the tendency or longing to escape from ordinary life into a relationship with the divine. For Grace, this gave rise to the danger of seeing herself as very different from others, inevitably alone and/or unable to have deep relationship as a result of the withdrawal of eros deep within.

This dream expresses Grace's highly individual and creative relation to the divine in particularly eloquent form. First of all, it is a very beautiful dream, unambiguously about God. Second, Grace's image of her relationship with God, a therapeutic relationship, suggests a way of viewing spiritual life that is meaningful to people who are theologically uneasy. The relationship with God that many of us were brought up with was an authoritarian one. God loves us, but God also has high and inflexible standards by which we are judged. It has been a part of the Christian tradition in some of its aspects to have, historically, emphasized our sinfulness and God's inevitable judgment to the exclusion of virtually everything else. To believe in the love of God, we need to experience the love of God. The real-life experience Grace has had that was closest to the love of God has been the experience of our relationship. And what better, more contemporary image of the love of God than God as the perfect therapist. God the perfect listener, God the all-wise advisor, God whose presence provides us with a strengthened container for ourselves, our feelings, our creativity, God who has no countertransference except selfless, unconditional love, God whose great power is used on our behalf. In *Primary Speech*, Ulanov uses the notion of primary process, those thoughts and feelings that arise from our deepest sources and form the basis of therapeutic/analytic work. She believes that our prayers need to come from that level, from the most fundamental level of experience. We need to be in dialogue with God about what really concerns us and not present ourselves to God in some sort of ego- or persona-based version. In order to do this, we need an image of God that is utterly trustworthy. In Grace's dream, she pours out her heart, her real concerns to God, and God hears her as the perfect therapist would hear her, the therapist who has the power not just to hear but also to heal. Analytic-based therapy shares with spiritual direction the sense that the therapist needs to be guided by the "third" in the room. In Christian spiritual direction, this presence is the Holy Spirit. In analytic therapy, it is the movement of both the client's and therapist's unconscious in the field of consciousness created in the therapeutic container. In Grace's dream, God is both the therapist and the spirit, a therapist entirely worthy of the most profound trust and love. In the therapist God, there is no distance between the kind of complete and selfless attention the therapist aspires to, the actual presence of the therapist, and the most profound contact with the divine.

The final dream is a recent dream of Grace's. Though she has continued to experience the presence of the divine in her dreams in various ways, this dream was the first dream in some time explicitly about God. And it was her final dream about God in our relationship. Grace's work with me is finished. She has moved on with her life to more creativity, deeper relationships and motherhood.

Working with God

I find myself in a large white room, an open space with a slanting roof, entirely composed of windows. It is an attic open to the sunlight that dazzles the room. There with me is a great broad man with a wild head of white hair, a rumpled face, and soulful brown eyes, wearing a white lab coat. He reminds me of a giant Einstein, and I know it has to be God. The way he looks at me at his side as he busily moves around the room makes me know that I am working for God, that I'm his assistant. Of course the real tip-off is that I'm also wearing a white lab coat.

God shows me what he made and what we two are working on, creating new beings. Lying on a bed, the bed I had as a child, are three figures. They look like wax baby dolls at first. As I step close to what kind of wonders God is up to I see that dolls are human and fleshy, and they aren't babies but baby-sized beings with adult bodies, both male and female. Their faces aren't worn, marred by time and hardship, but fresh and pure, like grown-ups who are magical babies again, and so are truly born again. They lie on the bed not breathing; but not dead, yet not alive. God tells me to get "the Animating Spirit." At least that is what I think he said. He said it in Latin, I suspect. I'm not sure, but I get the gist, and I certainly don't want to mess up, not on my first day on the job with God. I turn to God's cupboard, a lovely old oak Gothic dish cabinet that I inherited from my mother, something she loved but never fit in the house because it was too big, but it fits in mine. Through the glass of the cupboard I see rows of sparks of light. Oh, no. They all look the same to me. Yet, I know that they are all the spirits and forces that God possesses, and they all look identical. But one.

There is a warmer light, one that feels hot to me. "That must be the life force," I think. I take it out of the cabinet cupped in my hands, holding the light like a butterfly, one of fire but never burning. Right away I present the light to God. He looks at me sideways like I'm a bit of a goof. "That's not animating spirit," he says, "that's core of being." For a moment I know that the light I have is not what is going to bring these new beings to life. And as that knowledge reaches me, it wakes me.

Grace wrote a letter about her dream:

I woke with a wonderful feeling of being aligned with God. I had always thought that being a writer, being an artist of any sort, was to be in league with the divine, and also made one need to be in league with God. Since I had had no great success with my writing, no child, and no work had come to life, I always felt far from God. This dream told me different, and continues to make me feel different: there's a freshness and newness I feel all the time. I don't even feel the energy-killing grind of editing and checking my work as badly as before. I was born in the dream.

When I think about what the dream means, I quickly recall that all my life I'd struggled with "core of being." Always, the very center of myself was hidden from me, and often I thought it had been stolen from me. My mother used it. She ate my heart. What comes to mind is the time I first told her I was in therapy. She asked me what was wrong with me and I told her of my despair. She suddenly started to cry, and I thought it was for me. But she sobbed as she told me what her own analyst had found wrong with her: a sense of abandonment that she would never recover from. So, I had no knack of feeling for myself, or really knowing who I was, or feeling solid about that self-knowledge. Of course, dad was handy in the destabilization process. If I ever showed a spark of life, if I ever made anything he criticized it, and told me I was nuts or stupid. Usually both. He left when I was young, thirteen, and though he was wealthy, he made sure my mother and I didn't have enough. So I had to beg him for money, and went to get a part-time job at fifteen. My sister never defended me. And there were many, too many years which I spent pleasing people to get by, to survive. The dreams tells me I have done with that.

The dream also tells me I mistake "core of being" for the animating force. It's a mistake that brings hope to me for I now believe I am resolving my struggle to form the core of being and will be free to "see" other forces in God's cupboard, beginning with the animating spirit. That's what it will take to bring my work to life, to get it produced or published. And that's what it will take to have a child. That's what I need to come out into the world after so many years in my cloistered world of writing, for finding new friends, and enjoying and creating my new marriage and family. The dream was rich in that new energy. I think, too, the dream talks about my family. The clue to me here is that there are three beings to be born, and three is the number in my family; my mother, father and sister. Just recently, I reduced my ties to my last living relative, my sister, after years of bitterness and support—her bitterness and my support for her. I feel the dream says my ties with them, dead or alive, will change, will be born new as my life turns from "core of being" to face "the animating spirit."

And so I return to my writing knowing that I've developed rich, complex, honest characters who populate my stories, and provide my work with a number of "cores of being." I'll return to my desire to have a child with my hope reborn as faith. All I need is inspiration, energy, vitality, the essential magic of life.

In Grace's final dream and her commentary on it, we can see the growth that has taken place. Now Grace is God's assistant, a job description that applies to all of us. The divine needs us to embody it, to act for it. It needs human instruments to work in the world. And in order for us to fulfill that task, in order, to put it in Jungian terms, for the ego-Self axis to be well developed, we need a sense of core of being, through which can be channeled animating spirit. We can see this in terms of our abilities to both be authentic and creative, and help others. Therapists and spiritual directors talk about the presence of a third force in the personal relationship that characterizes these ways of working. Analysts and therapists often refer to the unconscious as if it were an autonomous being. Some analysts refer to the space between analysts and analysands as "the field" where something is created that is the result of the activities of the psyches of both analyst and analysand.

Spiritual directors talk about the will of God. However it is described, it is not accessible to or created by the will of either person in the relationship. It has a spontaneous life of its own, and it brings the capacity for consciousness and healing. We can also see it in terms of our inner development into whole persons. The spontaneous changes that occur in us as a result of, as Jung would put it, the transcendent function, or as Christians would put it, grace, comes to us more easily if we do not fear it, and having a well-developed core of being, which includes a sense of already being connected to the divine, is a great help in diminishing fear.

Grace is a woman who has always had access to her unconscious, but her work with her own dreams gave her greater access, and allowed the psyche to exercise its own tendency towards development and healing. Her work with her dreams removed her from the gelatinous murk of her enmeshment with her mother and made her God's assistant, which in turn gave her back her own life so that she could finally live it with the pleasure and energy she was capable of, giving and receiving love abundantly and living out her own creativity in the way that is most authentic for her.

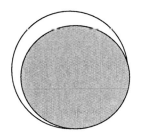

9
Transference and
Spiritual Connection

From a Jungian standpoint, it can be argued that all analytic and therapeutic work is a form of spiritual activity. Lionel Corbett takes the position that, since a great deal of human suffering is caused by the archetypes attempting to incarnate, even therapy that seems to be focused on issues that are not explicitly spiritual are nevertheless spiritual in the end. However, it is also true that there are points at which the work becomes explicitly spiritual: the client is consciously concerned with his or her relation to the divine. This is the stated focus of spiritual direction, and it can also happen in the course of analysis/therapy.

One of the features of a context that makes it possible for clients to approach the divine is the quality of the transference and countertransference. That is, with some clients and therapists/analysts/spiritual directors, the divine calls to the divine. In chapter 8, the story of Grace's essentially spiritual journey began with her having a sense of recognition when we met. It is my sense in such situations that there is a sense of spiritual "call" on the part of both client and therapist, a sense that the relationship is meant to be, that fate has brought them together. Interestingly, though Grace and I have had a long and rewarding relationship, she has seldom dreamt about me. I believe this is because, first of all, she has such a strong sense of following her own individual path, and she produces rich imagery that is uniquely hers. She has done both of these since she was a child. She did not need me in her dreams to stand in until she had created an image for herself. As well, she is conscious of relating to me as a spiritual mother and has been from the beginning; this does not have to be revealed to her in dreams. However, in my experience this is not typical. Usually, the relationship gradually develops a depth that allows the client to experience the therapist/analyst/spiritual director as a spiritual parent or spiritual guide. This is often necessary in order that the client deepen her or his relation to the divine: in the same way the therapist can "hold" the projection of the good parent until the client can internalize it, he or she can also "hold" the projection of the divine until the client develops her or his own relation to it. Eventually, this kind of relationship needs to be conscious to avoid the destructive possibilities inherent in it.[1] If it can be made conscious, it leads to a new dimension in the work.

In many myths, the hero has both a biological and a spiritual mother. The spiritual mother is a kind of spiritual midwife, who accompanies, nurtures, and challenges the hero in his struggles for transformation, maturity, and spiritual growth.[2] The relationship to a spiritual mother or father can be the determining factor for a stronger and deeper relation to the divine. In this chapter, I will discuss two dreams of clients in which I appeared as a spiritual parent, and one dream of my own in which my sense of spiritual "call" in working with a particular client was affirmed.

When she had this dream, Fran was a woman of forty-five with a long career in theater. I first worked with her in psychotherapy; Fran was my client. We worked for about two years, mainly with dream material, on issues having to do with life problems (she was married with one child), family-of-origin issues, and strengthening her sense of self. We had a very strong sense of connection, and the work we did together was useful for her and creative for me. I was away for a time, and during this time she did not continue in therapy with anyone else. Then, when I began to do spiritual direction in addition to psychotherapy, I found myself thinking of her and, as I often do when I find myself thinking about someone very persistently, I telephoned her to tell her I was doing spiritual direction and that somehow it had made me think of her. She was immediately enthusiastic, saying that spiritual direction felt like something she had been wanting for a long time.

In her first session in spiritual direction, we talked about her life: she and her husband were separating, she was feeling much stronger creatively, and she was feeling a need for some kind of spiritual life. Her background was Lutheran, but she was not interested in going back to church. She felt she needed something, some path, that was authentically hers. We decided to work with her dreams, in the hope that, just as her dreams had helped her develop a fuller life, so they would guide her in her spiritual development.

Fran began recording dreams of threatening and then of helpful numinous masculine figures. For her these images had meaning at all three levels. First of all, she was in the process of separating from her husband. She believed this was the right thing to do, but her feelings about it were complex and painful.

As well, she was coming to know the masculine in herself, some of which she had projected onto her husband, who was also in the arts. The dreams helped her bring her own issues around the masculine to consciousness and to live it out in ways not connected with her relationship to her husband. She also felt that she had always thought of the divine as masculine, and had projected this onto her husband as well. Her husband was an androgynous man who in the end felt himself to be gay, which was one of the major reasons for the breakup of their marriage. She believed that she had often projected spiritual qualities onto the gay men she had known. Her husband had in a sense carried her spiritual life through her conferring on him spiritual qualities.

Then explicitly spiritual imagery began to appear in her dreams: her son, wearing a T-shirt with an angel on it, and candles that would be appropriate for an altar. She began to work on bringing these images into her conscious life; she looked for angel imagery, made an altar with candles in her own home. She began to think about a spiritual practice. Then she had a powerful dream in which I appeared.

Fran and Bonnelle Climb the Mountain

I have seen a photograph of Bonnelle involved in native Indian spiritual practices. In this photograph, she is called "feather warrior woman," and I feel she is angry with me. We get together and talk about this, and resolve it. To prove we are still friends, Bonnelle invites me to meet her for dinner. When we meet, she asks me whether I like Mexican food. I say it's my favorite and she tells me she knows a special place in a hidden neighborhood where we can shop for food. Then she leads me up a hillside which gets steeper and steeper.

Bonnelle takes me into a house on the very top of the hill. We go into the bottom of it and then climb thousands of green stairs, surrounded by green glass windows through which we can see clouds; that's how high up we are. And through the clouds, we can see the city below. At the top of this eagle's eyrie of a house is a beautiful little kitchen, all gleaming and modern and full of green glass appliances. Even the cupboard doors are made of translucent green glass.

I think, "I love this kitchen." Bonnelle is busily opening cupboards and suddenly all this extraordinary Mexican food appears on green glass plates. I happily pick up a taco and perch on a high stool eating my favorite food and looking down at the city below.

This dream is about trust, about its place in the therapeutic relationship and in consequent spiritual life. It is also about the manifestation of the feminine aspect of the divine. It opens with Fran's fear that I am angry with her because she has discovered something about me that is at odds with her waking experience of my more public identity as Christian. It is also an image of Fran's relation with her own inner "wise woman"; Fran's earliest religious training was Christian, but she is presently attracted to spiritual practices from other traditions. It also contains evidence of our strong connection: though my spiritual formation was, and my commitment is, Christian, I have never had a dream that has specific Christian content (with the possible exception of the implicit reference to the identification with Jesus in my dark dream in chapter 6), such as a dream about Jesus or the Virgin Mary. I have, however, had several dreams with First Nations spiritual imagery. Mario Jacoby, in his book *The Analytic Encounter*, gives several examples of clients who dreamed about details of his life they had no way of knowing about.[3] Jacoby points out that when there is a strong psychic connection between client and therapist, one aspect of this connection can be between the unconscious of the client and the unconscious of the therapist. Fran had somehow connected to whatever it was in the religious function of my psyche that produced the First Nations spiritual imagery in my dreams.

In establishing that I am not angry with her, I do something in the dream that seems to be an image of what a great deal of our work together has been about: I invite her to dinner. Fran has experienced our relationship as nourishing from the beginning. However, this nourishment is more complex than simply satisfying an emotional need. In the dream, in order to get the food, we have to travel. We climb an increasingly steep hill and finally arrive at very unusual house, placed at the very top. We climb up and up the green stairs, looking out the green glass windows that surround them. We arrive finally in a wonderful kitchen. My own sense of this dream is that the climb up the hill represents the early part of our work: it was steep going, and it was about the basics of life. The hill is a natural object; climbing involves putting feet on the ground. Then there is a transition from the natural setting of the hill to the extraordinary house. The house has many layers of meaning. The house is high and transparent; it has many levels. When we get to the top, we're in the clouds and see the city below. This seems to represent Fran's complex, many-leveled ego and the development of the ego-Self axis. Though houses usually have solid walls, this house is full of windows and, at the same time, is still a solid structure. It reaches up, into the clouds. Fran can see through the walls into both the clouds and the city below. The walls of her ego are strong enough to contain her but also are transparent so that she can be in relation with the rest of the psyche and indeed the rest of the world. This lovely house both contains and is a vantage point. The greenness of the glass brings to mind the Emerald City of Oz and Hildegarde of Bingen's notion of *viriditas*, "greening."[4] Hildegarde used the notion of greenness to represent both physical and spiritual liveliness and health. Because Fran is inside the green building, she looks out over a green world and she is surrounded by green. She sees the world through a spiritual glass not darkly but greenly.

There is nourishment inside the building, nourishment that is just for her; her favorite food. This is an image of spiritual life that is an image of pleasure, nurturance, vision, and relationship. Though there is effort involved from the beginning—facing the possibility that I may be angry with her, climbing the hill and the stairs—it is not agonizingly painful. And it ends in a deeply pleasurable experience. This is an aspect of spiritual life that is often not sufficiently emphasized, especially by those who think of spiritual life as essentially ascetic or sacrificial in a negative sense. Yet even in the work of St. Theresa, who talks a great deal about suffering, there is an ongoing sense of being nourished by God and delight in God. In Fran's dream, I am her connection with the divine, the divine guide and mother, leading her to a beautiful place where she has her favorite food, just what she needs. Furthermore, she has a view; she can see the "big picture" while she is being nourished. Seeing the "big picture" is characteristic of the Self's point of view rather than the ego's.

The next dream comes from Simone, a client with whom I also had a particularly strong and deep connection. We worked together for some time, and as we worked through the painful life issues she brought, she seemed to move to a deeper place in both her own psyche and in her connection with me. She had a series of important dreams; the following dream seems especially appropriate for this discussion.

Simone Visits Bonnelle and Friends

I go out to the back of the Hotel Vancouver to meet Bonnelle. She's living in a house (cottage, really) attached to the hotel, which looks at the back like an Italian villa–all terra cotta and golden light. The cottage is small, very charming and with lots of fine handcrafting in the details. We sit at a picnic table in the garden. The garden is very lush and beautiful with many flowers. While we're talking, I admire the abundance of food that surrounds us on the table and on the garden wall. Such bounty: a chicken, a crab, many kinds of fruit, vegetables, and so on.

As we're talking, a rainstorm suddenly comes up. The rain (a warm, tropical rain) begins to pour down. Bonnelle begins to dance barefoot around the garden, reveling in the rain. I sit for a moment, not knowing quite what to do, watching B., then I notice that the rain is starting to run the ink on my dream notes, so I move out of the rain under the eaves where B. is not standing.

As B. and I finish our session, some friends of hers are there. All women, all very friendly and jovial. We had rushed to protect some of the food in the rainstorm, and all set about preparing it for dinner. I feel a part of the group; I feel that everyone's taking it for granted that I should be there, yet I feel a little awkward—I haven't actually been invited to stay, everyone's just assuming that I will. I wonder if I'm intruding at all on B. and her friends, although, apparently, they are very happy to have me there.

We all sit down to a wonderful meal. Although I'm loving the experience, I have another pang of worrying that I don't really belong there. I move to the far end of the table, away from B. My intention is to give her "space," but she looks at me and smiles, pats the seat beside her, and says, "Come here and sit by me."[5]

This dream was quite long and I edited it for the anthology in which it originally appeared. In a section of the dream that I left out, there is an archway into my garden with magical symbols carved on it.

Simone resembles both Grace and Fran, women whose spirituality is expressed not only through a sense of the presence of the divine in the inner life, but also a sense of the sensual world as being saturated with spirit. Pleasure, spontaneity, beauty, eating, and drinking, all have both a spiritual and emotional significance. She is also an instance of Lionel Corbett's important observation that the divine comes in through the wounded place, since this is the place where the barrier between the conscious and the unconscious is thinnest. The painful unconscious complex clamors for our attention through emotional distress and difficult functioning, and through it, the divine enters. In Simone's case, her natural vitality and hunger for meaningful life was systematically frustrated by her parents. Both were emotionally repressed, self-absorbed, and capable of a kind of passive cruelty through neglect. Sometimes they seemed almost to forget that Simone existed. When they remembered, it was her job to be "no trouble." She managed to survive this emotional and spiritual desert through withdrawal, splitting off and repressing her feelings. As a method of self-nourishment, her unconscious created beautiful, expressive, extraordinary dreams. Her life had been full of massive efforts to create something better for herself through work and relationship. She began therapy because she had been unable to find the kind of relationship she needed and because work had also become frustrating and difficult. Her profound unmet emotional and spiritual needs made spiritual mothering, in the sense of emotional and spiritual resources in the therapist that are available to the client, especially important.

In Simone's dream, I act as both helper and initiator. In coming to me for help, she is introduced to a different way of life, a sharp contrast to her lonely life with her emotionally stingy parents. In my garden, there is bounty. It is beautiful, it is nourishing, and there is companionship. She gets what she needs at every level and she's enjoying herself and life deeply. Life in the garden is a kind of lush green stream that she can plunge into. Everywhere she looks, there's something.[6] Again, one thinks of Hildegarde's *viriditas*. This is a profoundly feminine image of the divine: minimally hierarchical, sensual, inclusive.

It is interesting to notice the different roles that my character plays in the dreams of Fran and Simone. In Fran's dream I am troubling (she's afraid I'm angry), nourishing (I invite her to dinner), and guiding (I lead her into the green building). Both the nourishing and guiding roles are common roles of the divine in psychic life. The Christian tradition and others, as well, are filled with images of the divine both leading and prompting journeys and wanderings, and of the divine feeding the soul. However, there is also the role of being troubling. In the dream, Fran fears that I will be angry with her for knowing something about me that I have not directly revealed to her. She knows that I have a spiritual life that is different from the one with which she is familiar. She is afraid I do not want to be known by her. This fear of the wrath of the divine seems to be partly connected to our awareness of the otherness of the divine and the possibility of dangerous encroachment. Think of Adam and Eve. God told Adam and Eve they could have a wonderful life in the Garden of Eden and eat from any tree except the tree of knowledge of good and evil, a kind of knowledge apparently reserved for God. When they disobeyed this prohibition, they were exiled from Eden forever. Prometheus dared to bring fire from the gods to earth, and was chained to a rock and tormented for his hubris. In Fran's case, she wanted to know whether it was acceptable for her to know me in her own way, not in the way I presented myself at my office at the cathedral. She needed a connection to the divine that was not a submission to authority, but rather one that would bring forward something out of her own depths. Only when she was assured that this was possible was our journey upwards possible. I suspect that this particular anxiety about the divine is also connected to a family structure in which it is not possible to know one's parents in any way but the way in which they present themselves. Any picture but their picture is unacceptable. This was certainly the case in Fran's family.

In Simone's dream, I appear as unconventional (we have our session in the garden), bountiful (the garden is lush, there is plenty of food), connected to nature (again, the outdoor setting), living in a magical realm (the arch with the magical carvings), celebratory (dancing in the rain), and, in the end, inclusive and welcoming (I invite her to sit down). All of this imagery strongly suggests the feminine divine, the divine as connected to nature. I bring the possibility of nourishment, aesthetic pleasure, and companionship. However, there is also the moment of considering the otherness of the divine. She wonders whether she should be joining in the dinner with my friends, whether she is intruding. She moves down the other end of the table to give me "space." The question is similar to Fran's question: how does one approach and connect with the divine? In Fran's case, she moves toward me to solve the problem: we get together and resolve it. In Simone's case, she fears rejection and moves away, waiting to be invited. And she is invited, invited to join not only me but my friends, invited to join a feminine world of beauty, joy, pleasure, and connection. It is not surprising that Simone had to be invited; as with Fran, her experience with her parents shaped her expectations of the divine. Her parents made it clear that she wasn't very important, that their relationship to each other was more important than their relationship to her, and that there was barely room for her in the family; the condition was her being completely undemanding, "no trouble." She needed to feel that there was plenty of room for her and plenty of everything else, and that she was very welcome.

The philosopher Philip Hallie, in his book about the Holocaust, *Lest Innocent Blood Be Shed*, discusses the notion of cruelty as a vice and what the corresponding virtue might be.[7] He argues that cruelty is not just inflicting pain but also causing humiliation. He uses examples of how the Nazis humiliated the Jews, making them feel less than human. By the same token, the corresponding virtue is not kindness, which is available in momentary form even in concentration camps, but what Hallie calls hospitality: welcoming people, making them feel wanted and valued, and voluntarily renouncing the inequalities of power that make cruelty possible. Hallie states that cruelty is only possible in situations of inequality of power; it is difficult to persecute an equal, who needn't stand for it. Hospitality involves a renunciation of the advantages of inequality of power in favor of care. He uses as an example the people of the French village of Le Chambon, who successfully hid many Jewish refugees at great danger to themselves. The people of Le Chambon not only hid the Jews, but were hospitable towards them, glad to shelter and help people whom they viewed as God's chosen ones. This analysis of cruelty is transferrable to family life. Parents are in a position of absolute power from the child's point of view. If the child does not feel welcome, if she or he feels her or his acceptance is provisional, that she or he is a bother and a problem if she or he expresses any desires or needs, it is cruel, humiliating, and indeed, dangerous, in the deepest sense. It prevents a sense of worth from growing, and can create a feeling of shame about one's very existence. Such was Simone's family life.

There is a strong emphasis on connectedness in my relationships with both Fran and Simone. In both cases food is involved. Both Fran and Simone were emotionally undernourished in their families, both have a strong creative drive and are highly individual. Spiritual and emotional food for such women is often hard to come by. They can't "digest" the kind of nourishment offered in some religious traditions. This is particularly true in a religious tradition such as Christianity, in which sacrifice and austerity are often emphasized at the expense of nourishment and, historically, in which the feminine has been suspect and undervalued. Many Christians were brought up to believe that any interest in beauty and pleasure was somehow selfish and/or a temptation of the devil, and that women were inferior and even dangerous to the spiritual life of men. For these two women, this kind of spiritual "food" is useless. They need something that nourishes both emotionally and spiritually. They need loving connection rather than austere hierarchy. This sort of spiritual and emotional relationship with a therapist or spiritual director opens up the possibility of a similar relation to the divine.

Finally I want to discuss a dream of mine that indicates a spiritual connection with a client. This is the dream I had about Tiffany, discussed in chapter 7. I have already discussed the variety of meanings this dream had for me. What I want to emphasize now is the importance of my sense of spiritual connection with Tiffany.

Prayer for Tiffany

I am in a large room at the top of a building, a loft. I am wearing some kind of robe or toga. Tiffany comes in, draped in a sheet. She is in anguish, and she is supported on each side by a woman. At first she sits down on a couch, and begins to bend and writhe in agony. Then I signal the women to bring her over to a long table so that she can lie down. She stretches out on the table. I stand beside her and raise my arms to heaven in a gesture of prayer and supplication. The whole dream takes place in silence.

Often in my work with clients, I pay particular attention to whether the client seems to have a sense of spiritual connection with me.[8] This is invariably a consideration in spiritual direction, but it is also an important consideration in psychotherapy. A sense of spiritual connection with the spiritual director or therapist helps activate spiritual energy through encouraging hope for being genuinely understood and working in a context in which it is possible to develop and discover a sense of meaning in one's life. When people feel a sense of spiritual connection as well as empathy, there can be a sense that the relationship is in some way "meant," that one is on a path where assistance appears as needed, a path of grace. There is a saying that is attributed to various Eastern traditions: "When the student is ready, the teacher appears." This can also apply to relations between client and therapist, directee and spiritual director. In fact, if there is not this sense of "meantness" in both directions, there is a missing dimension.

The practice of psychotherapy and spiritual direction are hard work. They require patience, stamina, self-examination, and the ability to detach oneself from one's own agenda without abandoning the insights that come from one's own perspective. The work has meaning from many points of view: it is satisfying to be able to help, it is satisfying to see people grow, one learns a great deal about oneself, it is different every day so it is constantly stimulating. However, long-term work with seriously wounded people can also be punishing. One spends a great deal of time with people who are full of sorrow and rage, who often feel possessed by sorrow and rage. Sometimes after a session with such people, the therapist feels beaten up and left for dead by the intense experience of negative emotion. It helps a great deal if there is a sense that this client is part of one's own spiritual journey, that there is some meaning in the work for one's own spiritual development as well as the client's. This is one of the meanings of my dream about Tiffany. It showed me that I would have to rely on the divine in a way I hadn't before, that I would ultimately have to trust in the divine rather than my own experience and technical expertise. The dream takes place in silence. If the dream can be said to have a language, it is a language of movement. Tiffany is supported by two women; she writhes in agony; I lift up my arms in supplication as she lies on the altar. This is a difficult area for me; I have lived a great deal of my life as an intellectual, talking and teaching. That's what I'm especially good at. To be able to acknowledge my limitations, to ask for divine guidance in the face of an agony I cannot touch through talking and teaching, is spiritual growth for me. There was always a "meant" quality to Tiffany's relationship with me. There was an equally "meant" quality to my relationship with her.

In all of these instances, dreams played an important role in growth of awareness of the divine, and helping both my clients and myself to understand the depth and importance of our relationship to both of us. I felt honored by the dreams of both Fran and Simone; they told me that I had been able to make myself available to them in the way that they needed in order to feel nourished and to grow. My dream about Tiffany helped give me a stronger sense of the "rightness" of what I was doing, and the energy to continue even though I often felt consciously I was doing no good at all. This in turn helped Tiffany to develop faith in our process together and sustain our connection, even though she too often felt it was doing no good at all.

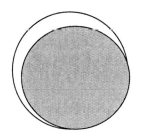

10
Coming Home

One of the major features of our spiritual lives is feeling. If we cannot make a feeling connection with whatever we consider our spiritual resources to be, we do not have access to the deepest aspects of our psyches. If we take seriously Jung's notion that the archetypes form the basis of the complexes that structure the psyche, we can see that affective connection must be a major feature in spiritual life. From a Jungian perspective, the archetypal core of complexes not only structures and draws specific kinds of images into the complex, it also carries strong affect. Complexes are both archetypal and specific to individuals; that is, the complexes have at their core common archetypal themes, but each of us has a particular version of these themes. One of the major sources of the experience of meaning is emotional connection, and the emotions that create this connection come from the complexes of the individual. These complexes are comprised of cultural and individual archetypally themed material. For example, someone brought up as a Christian will have been taught that Jesus is the only son of God and the savior of humankind and have various images that are connected to this teaching. Such a person will have learned this in a context that may have had a strongly emotional impact, which may have been positive or negative. For example, I have had several clients over the years who had very difficult family situations in which their needs for acceptance and belonging were not met. However, they were able to fulfill these needs by belonging to a church community in which they experienced themselves as valued and accepted. Thus their relation to the teachings of the church was extremely positive; the church offered them a substitute family with a highly idealized and loving parent (Jesus/God) at the center. On the other hand, I have also had clients who experienced their church communities in the same way they experienced their families:

demanding, perfectionist, and shaming. These feelings become connected with "being religious" through various archetypal routes: the authoritarian father, the neglectful mother, the dark, punishing Self. The people in the first example are likely to have had a continuous relation with a church community and experience their version of the divine as a positive and nourishing force in the psyche. The people in the second example are likely to have a great deal of difficulty with spiritual life, tending to see any relation to the divine as necessarily submissive, shaming, and destructive of their individuality. These are of course generalizations; religious experience can be much more mixed and ambiguous. Nevertheless, they demonstrate the origins and significance of emotional relations to religion. Spiritual formation is a complex process that also has a great deal to do with family life and the relation of religious life to the psychic dynamics formed by family life.[1]

Another important factor in making an emotional connection with spiritual matters is culture. In North America, we are in the interesting position of valuing both conformity and individuality. Both of these values have a long history in North American societies. Religious conformity has been a particularly strong value, and individuality has often been understood more in terms of responsibility than expression. That is, we are exhorted to be tough, ambitious, responsible for ourselves, and to not expect much from others, either individually or in the form of the state, in the way of assistance. This attitude has varied historically, and seems to be presently very much in the ascendency. However, another version of the value, somewhat less universally accepted, is the right to our own opinions and to live our lives the way we wish to. This value has a number of different manifestations, from the expression of creativity to a sullen resentment of authority. It currently plays an important role in spiritual life for many people. I have had many clients in both spiritual direction and psychotherapy who have experienced great difficulty making connection with any kind of spiritual tradition because they have such resistance to what they regard as stifling and critical authority. Their strongest association to religious life is the loss of their autonomy and individuality. For these people, it is essential to be able to have a sense that personal autonomy and individuality is highly valued in order to be able to be open to a spiritual resource.

For people who have a strong need to live a highly individualized and autonomous life, Jungian psychology can be moving and inspiring. Jung himself lived a highly individualized life in a strongly traditional and conformist society while maintaining a place in it. He continued to be creative in his own life up until the time of his death. His theories reflect his sense of the importance of individual life and offer a vision of the possibility of continuous creativity. Furthermore, he connects the development of individuality with relation to the divine. For Jung, the development of individuality is accomplished through inner work: self-knowledge, self-understanding, making what is unconscious conscious, knowing and accepting the whole self, and ultimately, through making a connection with the Self—the archetypal representation of the divine in the psyche—living out our individual lives guided by the Self. The very name of the spiritual path expresses individuality: individuation. For Jung, the path to spiritual life is through the inner life. Jung believed that spiritual life is essentially experiential: spiritual life that supports psychic development must be based on our individual experiences of the spirit. These may come through dreams, visions and creativity. From a Jungian perspective, there is no substitute for experience in spiritual life, particularly not through belief in the dogmas of a religious tradition simply because this is what one has been taught. This kind of belief is experientially deadening because it requires us to stifle our individual experiences and responses to these dogmas, and Jung saw these experiences and responses as, spiritually, the cutting edge. Emotional and imaginal experience and response is the manifestation of the archetypal core of the complexes that structure the psyche, and it is through emotional and imaginal response that we come to understand the unique manifestations of archetypal life in each of us. As I said in chapter 2, Jung believed the archetypes are the "organs of God";[2] because of the dynamic qualities of the archetypes, I prefer to think of them as the energies of God, at work structuring the psyche and providing each of us with the potential to make an authentic connection with the divine.

These views of Jung's have had great emotional impact on many people who feel spiritually stifled and blocked. Archetypally, Jung is often experienced as a kind of spiritual father and his writing has often provided a way into spiritual life through making people emotionally receptive to spiritual life as he describes it. It is his overall image of spiritual life as the deepest expression of the individual that provides this impact. This is in addition to the actual details of the theories themselves which, understood in an emotionally receptive frame of mind can offer the kind of profound experience of understanding and being understood and represented that is among the most satisfying forms of intellectual activity.

Does this mean that Jungian psychology is itself a kind of spiritual path? Yes and no, depending on what one includes in the concept of the spiritual path. Those Jungians who are particularly concerned with individualized spiritual life[3] emphasize spiritual life as contact with the energies of the Self in the psyche, the ego-Self axis. If the ego-Self axis is strong, our relation with Self will be vital and ongoing. We will experience imagery, synchronicities, dreams, and transpersonal emotions that enrich our everyday lives. We will experience our lives as meaningful because we will feel a strong connection to the divine in the psyche in such a way that we can see that the purposes of the divine are being served by difficulty and suffering and that our own increase of consciousness is an incarnation of the divine. This is clearly a rich spiritual life of a highly individualized kind. Just that fact that there is a psychological theory that can connect psychological and spiritual life is itself satisfying and can be healing for those who experienced spiritual life in childhood as rigid and having nothing to do with life as they have experienced it.

However, traditionally, spiritual life has existed not just through the individual's experience of the spirit, but also in the context of a relation with a larger tradition that provides other kinds of archetypally based experiences, such as ritual and teaching. Jung himself believed that one of the most satisfying ways to approach spiritual life was to return to the spiritual tradition that provided one's spiritual formation and understand it in a new way. From the standpoint of emotional and spiritual satisfaction, this seems to me to be true. In general, the more connectedness we can experience, the better off we are. The less we have to disconnect from our pasts, our families, or our cultures to have a satisfying life, the more accessible wholeness is. In addition, there is the question of the container for spiritual growth.

As discussed earlier, Jung's last work was in the area of alchemy. He believed that the alchemical process is an objective correlative of the transformation and growth of the psyche. Crucial to the alchemical process is the concept of the container in which the alchemical transformations take place. In the psyche, the container is provided by the Self, which contains the whole psyche. In the analytic process, the relationship between the therapist and client is the container for the transformation of both therapist and client, though the emphasis is of course on the transformation of the client. The analytic container allows the energies of the Self to be invoked for both client and therapist. The image of the container suggests that the energies of transformation need to be "held" while something new is taking shape, and that the presence of the container is essential to the process. The same is true of the specifically spiritual journey. While for a Jungian all inner work is spiritual since the complexes have an archetypal core, it is also true that some inner work is highly concentrated on the relation to the personal unconscious and strengthening the ego, while other work is highly concentrated on the ego-Self axis. It is this latter that constitutes the specifically spiritual journey. What containers are particularly appropriate to the spiritual journey? One candidate, already discussed, is the relation between the spiritual director and directee. This provides the same kind of container that is created by the therapist and client. Another candidate is a religious institution, such as a church.

There are many advantages to participating in a religious tradition. The liturgy enables us to experience an outward manifestation of an inward condition. We have the advantage of the experiences and insights of those who have gone before us. The church as container can connect us to the energies of the Self. There is another way in which the church can be a container, especially if the church is the institution that provided us with spiritual formation. The church can be a carrier of the archetypal energies of home.

Home is one of the most powerful archetypes in the psyche. It partakes of the archetypes of mother and father, but it is also strongly connected with the archetypal energies of the Self in the same way the alembic is alchemy. Edward Edinger has spoken eloquently about the relation of the alchemical vessel, in which transformation takes place, to the Self. The chemical transformations that take place are held safely and in a sustained way so that the process of transformation can take place. That home is a powerful archetype can also be seen in television commercials, real estate ads, and virtually every other form of advertising. It seems very likely that the longing for home is a multileveled desire which, in its most basic form, is a longing for physical safety and nourishment, and in its spiritual form is a longing for the divine. From a spiritual perspective, the divine is our soul's home. Many human activities—patriotism, the search for family trees and roots—have this archetypal core. The archetype of home is also an image of the relation between the stronger members and more vulnerable members of the family, Self and ego, between the divine and human beings. Home "holds" us; it is life giving and protective. From there we can negotiate the challenges and difficulties of human life, be nourished, be safe, trust that help and goodwill are at hand, and know we belong. Home is the venue for the most influential psychic transactions and transformations of our lives, and one of the major quests of human life is for home. A sense of being at home can provide us with the ability to trust and this in turn can help with reactive responses to spiritual resources as psychically dangerous authorities. Though many people have not found a home in the church, many have.[4] Is this, from a Jungian standpoint, bound to be suspect?

Jungians interested in the religious function of the psyche argue, with Jung, that living spiritual life through participation in organized religion can be spiritually deadening. This is because Jung believed that Christians traditionally lived their spiritual lives through projecting their inner spiritual activity onto Jesus and the church. Thus in a sense Jesus and the church lived their spiritual lives for them. Spirituality consisted in vicarious experience of Jesus's spiritual journey, and in some instances, those of the saints. The Bible contained all that was necessary for spiritual life, and one's individual spiritual experience was either irrelevant or suspect. Jung and contemporary Jungians such as Lionel Corbett argue that spiritual life is a natural activity of the psyche, and to be truly satisfying, it must be lived individually. Thus, to be part of a religious tradition is not only unnecessary, but perhaps even hazardous to individual spiritual experience. To see Jesus's spiritual journey as being more important than one's own is to fail to live one's spiritual life as deeply as possible. Instead, we must do our own inner work and attend to the numinous experiences that spontaneously arise. This work includes psychotherapy, analysis, and spiritual direction (Corbett believes psychotherapy is a form of spiritual direction), as well as spiritual practices such as contemplative prayer and meditation.

While it is certainly true that many people who participate in organized religion allow the church to define what is spiritually meaningful, this is not inevitable. It is possible to experience a particular religious tradition as meaningful to one's self and to have an active inner relation to it. For example, in Christianity it is possible to experience the presence of Jesus, and to see his life as a model for our own. We could say that we are not called so much to follow him as to *be* him. In addition, traditional spiritual practices, such as *conscience examen* and *lectio divina*, are inner activities that help develop one's individual relation to scripture and religious tradition. To actively engage with the liturgy[5] and seasons of the church can make us aware of how individual our relation to a religious tradition can be: Advent/Christmas and Lent/Easter can be different every year, depending on one's psychic and outer life. If one develops an inner relation to a tradition, one has the advantage of having both an inner life and being part of a larger community.

Another advantage of participating in a religious tradition is the rich resources it can bring to spiritual life. We need the help and inspiration of those who have come before. We need to wrestle with views we dislike to help build our own capacity for objectivity. And experientially, to be part of a larger religious community can replicate the ego's experience of being in relation to the Self. The church as a space and the liturgy as a structure in which all can participate forms a larger container for the individual. I do not mean the church as bureaucracy, but rather the church and liturgy as an experience. In the experience of liturgy, a psychic and spiritual "field" is created in the same way that it is created in therapy/analysis and spiritual direction. The spirit can be present among the participants in the liturgy and move them beyond themselves in the same way. It is a common experience for people who are regular churchgoers to come out of church feeling that their world has expanded, that the ego's point of view has been relativized, and that an interior process has led to a new point of view. The church and liturgy become outer manifestations of the structure of the psyche, with Self as container and center, and ego held there.

Both Jung and Jaspers were extremely uneasy about religious affiliation, though for different reasons. Jung was concerned that people saw Jesus's spiritual journey as the only one and allowed the church to live out the symbolic life for them, thus losing the opportunity for personal individuation and an authentic psychic and spiritual life. Jaspers believed that an adherence to revealed religion promoted prejudice and a misunderstanding of the nature of the Transcendent/Encompassing, which is limitless. Both Jung and Jaspers were intensely focused on the importance of the unique spiritual life of the individual, and what both considered the dangers and virtually inevitable lowering of quality of spiritual life that followed from adherence to any sort of doctrine. And they are not alone in these concerns. In my own work with directees and clients, as well as in giving workshops, lecturing and teaching, I have heard over and over how any connection with organized religion is bound to undermine a genuine spiritual life. Indeed, many people distinguish sharply between the spiritual and the religious. I have heard many people say, "I'm spiritual but I'm not religious." I find it interesting that it does not seem to occur to many people that there is anything limiting about this attitude. Perhaps this is because the usual criticisms of not joining religious organizations are theological—people who don't join don't see the light, haven't opened their hearts to Jesus, and so on—the very attitudes that create this heightened individualism to begin with. However, there are limitations to such heightened individualism.

Working with such people in psychotherapy and spiritual direction, I have often found that, while work with dreams and spiritual practice can connect them to the Self and be satisfying, there is also a frustrated desire for a spiritual home. In addition, there are the obvious limitations of one's own point of view. No matter how many books I may read, it is not equivalent to belonging to a spiritual community. As well, the view that one is enough for oneself spiritually might be said to lack humility. Surely we all need the spiritual assistance of others from time to time. As well, it's a lonely way to live one's spiritual life.

Many see Jungian psychology as a spiritual home, in that Jung affirmed the importance of spiritual life by redescribing it in psychological terms while at the same time avoiding reductionism: he gave spiritual experience a significance of its own, based on the phenomenology of human experience. Jungian theory and practice are a curious combination of analytic objectivity and the search for meaning that characterizes spiritual life. On the one hand, Jung's commitment to the phenomenology of the psyche, his notion that we should cultivate a conscious relation to our complexes and through this cultivate a closer relationship with the unconscious, offers us a picture of the uses of observation and detachment: that sliver of objectivity that can help clients work through the most painful material while owning it. The language of analysis is descriptive; the task of analysis is both understanding and healing, but both of these purposes can be described entirely descriptively. It is not a religious tradition in any ordinary sense: it has neither sacrament nor liturgy. On the other hand, the notion that the psyche is purposive, that its natural movement is toward the divine and that our dreams, fantasies, even our painful complexes are manifestations of the divine in the sense that the archetypes are the energies of the divine, is theology, and like the language of theology, the language of Jungian psychology is evocative and metaphorical. While Jung claimed to be a strict empiricist, his work with alchemy as well as his own psychic development strongly suggests that he sought meaning as well as information. The work of Edward Edinger and Lionel Corbett is unabashedly theological. Thus while Jungian work is conducted essentially as a relationship between two people, the context of Jungian work is much larger and becomes for many a spiritual home. They are not alone in their relation to the divine; they have the whole body of Jungian thought and its validation of the importance of individual spiritual life to ground them. The advantage of a Jungian ground for spiritual life is its emphasis on the importance of individual experience and the respect it engenders for one's own experiences without having to fit them into a framework of meaning that might or might not be appropriate. The disadvantage is the lack of tradition, ritual, and communal life that gives one opportunities for growth, both in oneself and in community. For example, the liturgy brings us home if we participate in it consciously and not automatically. We can return from our often scattered and busy external lives to our relationship with the Self. There is a strengthening sense of shared values, of commitment to a common vision of the spiritual life, and the possibilities for spiritual development that exist in relationships with people of like mind and values. There is also a model for our relationship to the world that goes beyond increased consciousness to doing good.

There is an additional sense of home for those who participate in the religious tradition that has provided their spiritual formation. Their changing relation to this religious tradition mirrors their own spiritual growth, and the experience of continuity provides a sense of rootedness and promotes the experience of our whole historical selves which is in itself affirming. This assumes, of course, that one participates in a version of religious tradition that supports individual spiritual life. This varies a great deal within Christianity, and in other religious traditions as well. Theologically, what is required is the belief that the spirit can manifest itself in many ways and still be genuine. As we have seen in our examination of dreams, the unconscious is no respecter of orthodoxy and it is not unusual for people who are deeply committed to a particular religious tradition to have dreams that draw heavily on the religious images of other traditions.[6] For example, though my own spiritual formation is Christian and my own active spiritual life is Christian, as I've mentioned, I have never had a dream that contained divine imagery that was explicitly Christian, with the possible exception of the implicit reference to Jesus in the dream I described in chapter 6. When I was in the process of returning to the Christian tradition after a long absence I had three important dreams with divine imagery, all of which drew on First Nations imagery. Here is the second, and clearest, of these dreams.

Coming Home

> I am walking home, walking along the sidewalk upon which I walked home from both elementary school and high school. It is completely recognizable as the street on which I grew up. I'm about two blocks from home. I'm walking, but I also see my back. It seems to be spring. The trees are arching overhead, and they are a beautiful yellow-green. They form a high, dense arch. The sidewalk seems more like a path, and is completely covered with pollen and the air is glowing and filled with pollen. There's a sense of being both at home and out of time.

When I had this dream, I had only the vaguest of memories of having heard somewhere, perhaps in the mysteries of Tony Hillerman, about the Navajo image of the pollen path as the spiritual journey. I had no conscious memories of any details. This dream illustrates the resourcefulness of the unconscious, perhaps even reaching into the collective unconscious for an image that would fit for me: I am going home, home to the tradition that has meant so much to me, and I'm going home with my own, fresh, green relation to it. The shadow side of the dream is implied rather than explicit: I grew up literally in the house my father grew up in, the house my grandfather built. So I'm going home to the house of my fathers, and this will be a challenge. But it is also true that, since my father died when I was young, my home was also a house of women, the home of my mother and sister and the place where black women worked for us, another dark part of the past. The important thing is that my spiritual journey is both a journey towards what is mine and familiar, and a journey on a strange path, a pollen-covered path which is unfamiliar yet beautiful and green.[7] One cannot help thinking, again, of Hildegarde's *veriditas*, the greening of the world, the enlivening of the world. Thus my relation to my own religious tradition is not a dead one. I may be returning to the ground of my original spiritual formation, but I am not allowing my spiritual life to be lived for me. I have my own individual relation to it. As long as I do, it will be a green path. Jung would have been sympathetic to the version of return offered in T. S. Eliot's *Four Quartets*:

> We shall not cease from exploration
> And the end of all our exploring
> Will be to arrive where we started
> And know the place for the first time.[8]

The Jungian relation to the past and our own history is a relation of depth, not distance. One can argue that we must at least come to terms with our own spiritual formation at some point. But further, there is a real sense in which our spiritual formation is a deep part of who we are. To repossess this at a deeper level seems a way of owning our personal history and identity, of actively engaging in our own histories. It has been my experience both personally and professionally that many people flee the traditions that have formed them, idealizing other traditions which are difficult for them to understand deeply because of cultural and historical differences. This is, of course, not always the case when people change traditions. However, it is useful to keep in mind that traditions and myths born in other cultures have the glamor of strangeness without the disadvantages of one's having lived out their consequences in the cultures that have formed and been formed by them. The most desirable relation to one's own history and the culture in which it occurred, when possible, is love. Without love, one is deeply alienated from something in oneself. It need not be uncritical love; indeed, there are forms of love that are challenging and difficult .⁹ This love for what is one's own is in addition to the love of God, and supports it. It assists us in forming the ego-Self axis, or to put it in religious language, welcoming the will of God as opposed to going along with it—an important spiritual task.¹⁰

Thus, though many contemporary Jungians seem to feel that participation in a religious tradition is a dangerous business, it is no more dangerous from a psychic or spiritual standpoint than the alienation from one's own past and from a larger spiritual community that occurs when one is cut off from one's religious past. Interestingly, many people who would not dream of recommending that we disconnect ourselves from our emotional or intellectual pasts are much more willing to consider some sort of absolute rejection of our religious past.

Both living spiritual life outside a religious tradition and inside a religious tradition can be done individually. Both are full of opportunities for inauthenticity, spiritual drift, and lack of depth. Both are equally full of opportunities for spiritual nourishment and growth. In the end, the choice we make may be partly temperamental. Gary Snyder's description of the poet's choices also holds true for the devotee of the inner life: "Comes a time when the poet must choose: either to step deep in the stream of his people, history, tradition, folding and folding himself in the wealth of persons and pasts; philosophy, humanity, to be richly foundationed and great and sane and ordered. Or, to step beyond the bound onto the way out, into horrors and angels, possible madness or silly Faustian doom, possible utter transcendence, possible enlightened return, possible ignominious wormish perishing."¹¹

These are choices of ways of life, and within each of these ways of life one can find a bit of the other. Clearly Jung chose the latter, but he was also deeply involved in European intellectual and spiritual traditions and practices; for example, his later writings exhibit his profound interest in and individual understanding of alchemy, and throughout his writings he makes frequent references to philosophers, theologians, scientists, and writers of every kind.

He was able to make his own tradition new for himself while taking enormous psychic risks. It is his unique ability to combine tradition and originality that is one of the most moving aspects of Jung's work. By the same token it is possible for someone to be devoted to one's own tradition and, at the same time, through inner work such as dream work, "step beyond the bound onto the way out, into horrors and angels."

Perhaps it would help if, in our communal religious experience, we made more public mention of dream life. I have met with surprising enthusiasm every time I have offered the opportunity for dream work at my church and at workshops and retreats. Dreaming about the divine is not an uncommon experience. It might be said that my own experience with clients is not typical, but I suspect that these dreams are more common that might be supposed. Jaspers argues that boundary situations are a feature of human life, and I have yet to meet anyone who has not experienced a considerable amount of suffering. We might remind ourselves at this point that the dreamers discussed throughout this book were often moved to dream about the divine through their woundedness, through having encountered boundary situations in severe forms. Experiencing these boundary situations caused the dreamers to connect with deeper emotional issues, to experience their particular places of woundedness so that, emotionally, they were more open to experience the divine. As Corbett argues, and as discussed earlier, the experience of the divine comes through places of woundedness in the psyche because the border between conscious and unconscious is thinnest there. Jaspers saw boundary situations as opportunities for the elucidation of Existenz, in particular as presenting opportunities for communication both with others and with oneself. From a Jungian standpoint, we might say that boundary situations stir up the psyche, touching into the affect and imagery of the complexes, not allowing us to hide from ourselves. And when we are stirred up in this way, we are often particularly receptive to many forms of experience of the divine.

Like Jung, Jaspers believed there was an aspect of our being that came from the divine, and like Jung he did not believe our experience of the divine was limited to the experience of organized religion. Jaspers calls the divine both Transcendence and the Encompassing. "Transcendence" expresses the aspect of the divine that is beyond our ability to experience directly, beyond the physical world, and so on. The Encompassing has to do with the divine as the infinite rather than its individual appearances. In either case, we can never experience the divine. What we can experience, according to Jaspers, are ciphers of the divine. The concept of cipher is very close to what Jung meant by symbol, though Jaspers did not have Jung's views about archetypes.[12] What Jaspers did have in mind was the experience of the divine, which he called ciphers of the Encompassing, whenever and wherever possible. He believed that anything could be a cipher, could be imbued

with meaning. And presumably for Jung, given the right psychic circumstances, anything can be a symbol, though of course Jung's emphasis when he
talks about the symbolic life is on the sorts of things that present themselves as
symbols, such as dream material, and the universal symbols of the great religious traditions. The reason Jaspers is helpful here is that he emphasizes, as I
think Jung wants to, the living of a certain kind of divinely saturated life
rather than channeling spiritual life just toward going to church, belonging to
a particular organization, subscribing to a certain set of theological principles,
and so on. Both Jung and Jaspers were concerned with the quality of our
experience of life, and the way in which this experience expanded our creativity, insight, and understanding into the kinds of beings we are and an
enhanced contact with the ground of our being. Interestingly, this concern
with a particular kind of spiritually saturated life moved both Jung and Jaspers
to oppose organized religion on different grounds. Jung believed that we have
a tendency to project our spiritual lives, for example, on Jesus and the church.
Jaspers believed that belief in revealed religion led to claims of exclusivity
which in turn led to bigotry and intolerance. While both of these claims can
be true, I would argue that neither need be true, though avoiding them can
be difficult. My own sense is that, at the present time, we may be at a turning
point in our relations to spiritual tradition. Many people have fallen away
from the traditions in which they experienced spiritual formation, whereas
many people have returned in a new way. Phenomenologically, a sense of
strong growth in the life of the spirit gives rise to a powerful desire to be
more engaged with the divine in community. This has left many people in a
painful spiritual quandary.

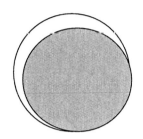

11

Dreams: The
Divine Connection

Dreams seem so ordinary. We dream from the time we can remember, and the effect of this constant accompaniment can be a kind of trivialization. We can come to scarcely notice our dreams and if we do, we don't make much of them unless they're in some way remarkable—beautiful, frightening, or awe inspiring. Yet the phenomenon of dreaming itself is truly remarkable. If we attend to it, we are reminded of our status as beings who are connected to a source beyond ourselves. The phenomenon of dreaming offers us a gentle, persistent, nonthreatening reminder that we are more than the busy self of daytime. And these dreams of the divine remind us, as Jung and Jaspers tell us, that we are more than our worldly selves. The divine shows itself in us at night, in forms that are unique to each of us, in forms that are often quite mysterious yet revelatory if we are willing to engage with them. Whereas not everyone seems to have access to mystical experience, dreams offer everyone an experience of otherness, sometimes profound and transcendent otherness. To engage with our dreams can be part of the elucidation of Existenz if we choose to live our lives consciously and authentically. They contribute to the kind of understanding of ourselves and of life itself that allows us to make choices to live deeply and fully. Jaspers saw Existenz as a gift from the Transcendent, and we can see what natural allies Jaspers and Jung are when we think of how the understanding of dreams reveals us to our conscious selves and develops our understanding of our hidden depths through communicating (as Jaspers would say) the activities of, in Jungian terms, the Self. Indeed, the activity itself of work on dreams, the self-attending that is involved in discovering and unpacking the meaning of dreams, helps us develop ourselves; it assists in what Jaspers calls our self-becoming. It helps us cultivate a sense of our own depths since it can lead us to a focus similar to contemplation and prayer. We enter a realm of meaning unlike the common-sensical and often practical meanings of the waking world, a realm that often has an alien "feel." We wait attentively for images and feelings to show themselves, for something from deep within to speak. We may actively pursue an image as it eludes us, but this is a focused watching: we stare into the bottom of the pond, trying to catch the movement of the fish. We become aware that there are sources in us that have their own life and operate on their own time, and experience the change in sense of being that comes when we make paying attention to those sources a part of life rather than living in a constantly reactive mode.

As well, dreams give us a way to help struggle with the problem of individuation and community in spiritual and religious life. It is my strong sense that we need both. As it stands now, it seems to me that a great many people seem to fall into one of two categories. On the one hand, there are those who belong to religious groups who hold rigid opinions from which there can be no variation and which do not welcome an individually lived spiritual life within a religious commitment. On the other, there are those who want nothing whatsoever to do with any sort of organized religion on the ground that it violates their individualized spiritual life. Neither of these positions seem to me satisfactory. Particular fundamentalist versions of the former are at the moment self-evidently problematic on a worldwide scale. The latter is problematic in the sense that it deprives those who hold it of important ways of finding their relation to the divine.

In all of the major religious traditions, we are asked in one way or another to let go of the ego. In the Christian tradition, Jesus says, "Not my will, but thine be done." In a secular version of this, Jung speaks of the ego-Self axis, the relativization of the ego. Anyone who is on a spiritual path is familiar with this, the desire, the struggle, the quest to do the will of God. And anyone who is on a spiritual path and who is familiar with this will also know how puzzled, how confused, how absolutely in the dark one can feel about whether one is doing this. Over a lifetime of relationship with God, most of us ask ourselves again and again what that relationship is, how we see that relationship, how indeed we see God. And to be spiritually nourished we need to be connected to as many spiritual resources as possible. However, because of concerns about fundamentalism and because until fairly recently some form of religious conformity has been the rule rather than the exception, many are correctly concerned with theological openness and nonrigidity.

In chapter 10, I discussed the connection with religious tradition as a kind of going home. But going home does not mean going home, shutting the door, and closing the windows. Going home has to do with finding ground to stand on and community to be in relation with and, in an inner sense, it has to do with finding a home in oneself, finding an authentic spiritual path to follow and finding a home in the divine; in Jungian terms, it has to do with committing oneself to the process of individuation. Spiritual life ought never to be seen as completed. The constant new life in work with dreams helps prevent that false sense of completion. We are living in a time in which the life of the spirit may be found in many places and needs to be continually sought even though one may have found one's home. My own sense is that theological rigidity and even just dullness has caused the life of the spirit to spring up in many places outside theology and the church. As Jaspers points out, ciphers are everywhere. As I have argued, certainly they appear in the world of dreams. In the previous chapter I mentioned the misgivings of Jung and Jaspers about organized religion, and those misgivings are well-founded. Jung and Jaspers push very strongly for a highly individual relation to life itself and the life of the spirit in particular. However, there may be other possibilities. To offer a contemporary example, in the collection of essays *A Passion for the Impossible*,[1] a tribute to the work of John Caputo, we can see a way of doing theology/philosophy that could accommodate both a subjective relationship to the divine and a commitment to a tradition while at the same time expressing the impossibility of any sort of absolute knowledge and the importance of not engaging in the illusion of finalization of belief. Jung and Jaspers are both pushing, so to speak, outward, out of any sort of commitment to organized religion. However, Caputo, partly through his work on Derrida, offers a version of our relation to "the Impossible," avoiding both orthodoxy and disconnected individualism. What particularly interests me is his approach, which includes the desirability and/or the capacity to both have a deep, authentic inward spiritual life and a commitment to a religious tradition. Caputo's work in this area seems very helpful and suggestive.

Our work on the spirit can take many forms and there are two main reasons why this must be so throughout our lives. I have said that it is important not have a false sense of spiritual life as completed and known, to keep it fluid and alive. Perhaps both of these reasons are obvious, but both are worth making clear, especially as they both bear on the importance of dreams. First of all, as Caputo (with Derrida) tirelessly points out, the transcendent is "the Impossible." We can never know the divine; we ought not to try to make the divine into something we can name and limit but this does not mean that we do not continue to long for the divine, to represent the divine humbly and, so to speak, not-knowingly in our longing. If we are open, we may be as fortunate as some of the dreamers in this book, and the Impossible may become momentarily possible, though of course not total and complete. We have only a glimpse, and are happy to have that glimpse. Second, because we are

constantly changing and a living relation to the divine is just that—a relation—our relation to the divine is constantly changing. What is emphasized
in our relation to the divine now may not be emphasized next year or even
tomorrow. Again, dreams can help show the way. In some dreams, the divine
appears as comforter because this is where the divine is most needed. In some
dreams, the divine is terrifying because the ego-Self axis is forming and the
ego needs to be challenged, not soothed. The psyche is constantly in process.
Dreams help us understand the essential transforming role the divine plays
from within as opposed to being something external to us, only to be visited
on Sundays.

Perhaps it seems odd to say that something so unsacramental as dreaming
could play an important part in keeping spiritual life alive, yet it seems to be
so. Dreams give us a direct connection to the divine. They are the paradigm
of the involuntary. They are our own voice of the divine that never stops
speaking. Our dreams can inform us continuously of our own individual relation to the divine even as we participate in the religious tradition to which
we are committed. Sometimes, as in the case of Jim, my client who dreamed
on Good Friday that he was humiliated by police interrogation, our dreams
make our relation to our religious tradition vivid and alive in a way that
nothing else could do. Jim was himself so humble that nothing but a dream
could have allowed him to think of himself as walking in the footsteps of
Christ. Sometimes our dreams enrich our relation to our religious tradition,
so the symbolism that is missing in waking life appears in our dreams. I think
of Grace, who dreamed she was having therapy with a God who was a grand
old man with a beard—the patriarchal God who was a poet, a philosopher,
and a therapist, the God who was not represented in her Unitarian tradition
and a patriarchal God in a form she could accept. Dreams are in a sense the
individuation fail-safe. We need not fear being lost or devoured spiritually by
the tradition in which we participate if we attend to and work with our
dreams, because they will provide the images we need to preserve our individuality. They will show us the individual version of the divine that we
require, they will tell us what is missing in our relationship with the divine
that will make it truly personal and meaningful to us, and, in many instances,
they will provide healing and nourishment in the existential crises of our lives
that Jaspers calls boundary situations, those situations that are inevitable: struggle, suffering, guilt, death, disappointment, and loss.

Dreams are extraordinary gifts that are given to us which we often continue to sleep through even when awake. Yet if we attend to them and
engage with them, both the dreams themselves and the process of coming
into relation with them can bring enormous psychic and spiritual growth.
One of my favorite prayers in the Anglican liturgy has always been the doxol-
ogy that comes after communion. This is the beginning:

Glory to God
whose power, working in us,
can do infinitely more
than we can ask or imagine.[2]

I particularly like this part of the prayer because it expresses so clearly what seems to me most important to remember: the divine can do infinitely more than we can ask or imagine. It is beyond our wills and wishes and efforts. However, it is also true that we may be in contact with the divine, this powerful force that can do more than we can ask or imagine, and dreams are a way that has been given to us to have that contact.

When I first joined Christ Church Cathedral, I gave a series of dream groups for the parishioners there, and on the first night of my first dream group, one of the members asked me if I thought that the voice of the Holy Spirit could be heard through dreams. Unhesitatingly, I replied, "Yes." This was many years ago, long before I began this book and began collecting dreams about the divine, and afterwards I was a little surprised at my lack of hesitation. But even then it was clear to me that there was divine energy in dreams and that through that energy, when we engage with our dreams, they can do infinitely more than we can ask or imagine towards enriching our spiritual lives and our connection with the divine.

Notes

Introduction: Point of View

1. James Hall, "Introduction: Unconscious Christians," in *The Unconscious Christian* (Mahwah, N.J.: Paulist Press, 1993).

2. While puttering around the edges of Buddhism, I met a number of spiritual exiles. Buddhism seems to me to be especially welcoming to spiritual exiles and wanderers. It emphasizes practice rather than theology, thus offering the opportunity to discover the essence of spiritual life, spiritual experience.

3. For the complete text of this dream, see C. G. Jung, *Memories, Dreams, and Reflections* (New York: Vintage Books, 1989), 11–13.

4. Jung, *Memories, Dreams, and Reflections*, 39.

5. Because Jung had a theory that was meant to account for general features of the human condition, a number of people have made connections between Jung's views and various philosophical views. Some I have found especially interesting are Roger Brooke, *Jung and Phenomenology* (London: Routledge, 1991); Sean Kelly, *Individuation and the Absolute* (connecting Jung and Hegel) (Mahwah, N.J.: Paulist Press, 1993); Marilyn Nagy, *Philosophical Issues in the Psychology of C. G. Jung* (Albany: State University of New York Press, 1991); and Petteri Pietikainen, *C. G. Jung and the Psychology of Symbolic Forms,* (connecting Jung and Cassirer) (Helsinki: Annales Academine Scientiarum Fennicae, 1999). As well, in the final chapter of *The Unconscious Christian,* James Hall offers an extended comparison of the epistemologies of Jung and Michael Polyani. Currently, Wolfgang Giegerich in *The Soul's Logical Life* (Frankfurt: Peter Lang, 2001) offers a Hegelian critique of Jung and Jungians. And no doubt there are others.

1. The Divine

1. *The Listener,* January 21, 1960, as cited by Dr. J. Glenn Friesen, "Jung, Ramana Maharshi and Eastern Meditation" (http://members:shaw,ca/jgfriesen/ homepage, Dr. J. Glenn Friesen, Calgary, Alberta).

2. C. G. Jung, "Bruder Klaus," in *Psychology and Religion,* CW 11 (Princeton, N.J.: Princeton University Press, 1958).

3. For a thorough discussion of these mystical aspects of Bion and Lacan as well as others, see Michael Eigen, *The Psychoanalytic Mystic* (Binghamton, N.Y.: esf Publishers, 1998*)*.

4. Karl Jaspers, *Philosophy*, trans. E. B. Ashton (Chicago: University of Chicago Press, 1970), vol. 2, 177–222.

5. Kurt Salamun, "Jaspers," in *A Companion to Continental Philosophy,* eds. Simon Critchley and William R. Schroeder (Malden, Mass.: Blackwell, 1998), 217.

6. Jaspers, *Philosophy,* 206.

7. For an excellent discussion of Jaspers's concept of the elucidation of Existenz and other Jaspersian matters, see Elisabeth Young-Bruehl, *Freedom and Karl Jaspers's Philosophy* (New Haven: Yale University Press, 1981).

8. Sigmund Freud, "The Uncanny" in *The Uncanny,* trans. David McClintock with an introd. by Hugh Haughton (New York: Penguin, 2003).

9. For a useful discussion of the notion of the satisfaction of desire, see Richard Wollheim, *On the Emotions* (New Haven: Yale University Press, 1999), 1–68.

2. Some Basic Considerations

1. Simone de Beauvoir, *The Ethics of Ambiguity,* trans. Bernard Frechtman, 7th ed. (Secaucus, N.J.: Citadel Press, 1975).

2. In the upcoming sections, there will be a number of references made to various philosophers. For those who are interested in the history of philosophy, I can wholeheartedly recommend the multivolumed history of Western philosophy by F. C. Copleston. F. C. Copleston, *A History of Philosophy*, vols. 1–9 (New York: Image Books, vols. 1–6, 1993; vols. 7–9, 1994).

3. Augustine, *Confessions,* trans. R. S. Pine-Coffin (Harmondsworth: Penguin, 1961).

4. De Beauvoir, *Ethics of Ambiguity*, passim.

5. The distinction between the voluntary and the involuntary forms the basis for Ricoeur's book of the same name. However, I am not making the distinction in the same way, or to the same end.5. For those with an interest in Hellenistic philosophy, I recommend A. A. Long's excellent book Hellenistic Philosophy (Berkeley: University of California Press, 2003).

6. For those with an interest in Hellenistic philosophy, I recommend A. A. Long's excellent book *Hellenistic Philosophy* (Berkeley: University of California Press, 2003).

7. For detailed discussions of the connections between emotional and spiritual life, see Lionel Corbett's discussion of the connection between Kohutian selfobject development and spiritual life in Lionel Corbett, *The Religious Function of the Psyche* (London: Routledge, 1996) chapter 2. Also see Ann Belford Ulanov, *Finding Space* (Louisville, Ky.: Westminster John Knox Press, 2001); Ana Maria Rizzuto, *The Birth of the Living God* (Chicago: University of Chicago Press, 1979); and Mary Wolff-Salin, *No Other Light* (New York: Crossroads Press, 1986).

8. See especially Iris Murdoch, *The Nice and the Good* (London: Chatto and Windus, 1969); Iris Murdoch, *A Fairly Honourable Defeat* (London: Chatto and Windus, 1970); Iris Murdoch, *An Accidental Man* (London: Chatto and Windus, 1971); and Iris Murdoch, *Nuns and Soldiers* (London: Chatto and Windus, 1980).

9. C. G. Jung, "The Transcendent Function," The Structure and Dynamics of the Psyche, CW 8 (Princton: Princeton University Press, 1960).

10. Eigen, *Psychoanalytic Mystic.*

11. For an extensive discussion of religious dreams in Western culture, see Kelly Bulkeley, *The Wilderness of Dreams* (Albany: State University of New York Press, 1994).

12. Rizzuto, *The Birth of the Living God.*

13. Ann Ulanov, for example, argues that "the Self...is neither spirit nor God per se but that within us which knows about God or the spirit." Ann Belford Ulanov, *The Functioning Transcendent* (Wilmette, Ill.: Chiron Publications, 1996), 24. This would make the relationship between the Self and the divine essentially epistemic and not necessarily participatory.

14. C. G. Jung, *Letters*, eds. G. Adler and A. Jaffe. Trans. R F. C. Hull (Princeton, N.J.: Princeton University Press, 1954), vol. 2, 130.

For extended discussions of the Jungian approach to spiritual life, see also Corbett, *Religious Function of the Psyche,* the works of Edward Edinger, particularly Edward Edinger, *The Creation of Consciousness* (Toronto: Inner City Press, 1984), the works of John Dourley, particularly John Dourley, *A Strategy for a Loss of Faith* (Toronto: Inner City Books, 1992); and the works of Janet Dallet, especially Janet Dallett, *When the Spirits Come Back* (Toronto: Inner City Press, 1988) and Janet Dallett, *The Not-Yet-Transformed-God* (York Beach, Me.: Nicolas-Hays Inc., 1998).

15. E.g. Edinger, *Creation of Consciousness;* Corbett, *Religious Function of the Psyche*; and Dallett, *When the Spirits Come Back and The Not-Yet-Transformed God.*

3. Dreaming about the Divine

1. Corbett, *Religious Function of the Psyche, p.16.*

2. Jung, "Bruder Klaus," *Psychology and Religion*, CW 11.

3. Ulanov, *Functioning Transcendent*, 24.

4. Eigen, "Musings on O" and "Serving Jouissance," *Psychoanalytic Mystic.* Since the divine is always beyond our conceptions, we might say that O and jouissance reveal to us a ground of being which is also other and are not as likely to mislead us into thinking we "know" the divine in some definitive way as images might be prone to do. For a useful discussion of our relation to otherness and its limits, see Mark Dooley, ed., *A Passion for the Impossible* (Albany: State University of New York Press, 2003).

5. See, for example, Julian's dream of Satan in Julian of Norwich, *Julian of Norwich: Showings,* trans. Edmund Colledge, O. S. A. and James Walsh S. J. (New York: Paulist Press, 1978), 311.

6. Hall, *The Unconscious Christian*, passim.

7. "Fragile areas of the personality are precisely those to which the numinosum will address itself, because they are where healing is most needed and where the barrier to the unconscious is most tenuous, so that pressure from the unconscious is felt most keenly." Corbett, *Religious Function of the Psyche*, 33.

4. Dreams of Help, Comfort, and New Life

1. "Look at the birds in the sky; they do not sow and reap and store in barns, yet your heavenly Father feeds them. Are you not worth more than the birds? Can anxious thought add a single day to your life?...Consider how the lilies grow in the fields; they do not work, they do not spin; yet I tell you, even Solomon in all his splendor was not attired like one of them." Matthew 6:26–30. The Revised English Bible (Oxford: Oxford University Press and Cambridge University Press, 1989) New Testament, 5.

2. Matthew 7: 7–8, Revised English Bible, New Testament, 6.

3. "Some contemplatives...maintain that all attachments should be sacrificed save one, the attachment to God. But others, such as Meister Eckhart, would say that there comes a time when even attachment to God must go. The reasoning behind this is that people must make an image, an object, a *thing*, of whatever they are attched to, and this creates insoluble problems. To make an image of God and to deal with it as if it were God is necessarily to reduce the realilty of God and to shut out some of the absolute mystery of God's nature. To become attached to such an image is eventually bound to result in some degree of idolatry. Although images can be helpful vehicles in the course of spiritual practice and insight, attachment to them will produce distortion." Gerald May, *Will and Spirit* (San Francisco: HarperSanfrancisco, 1987), 239.

4. Though the spirit world is represented as a house of ghosts, I think it is plausible that this comes from Laura's Catholic childhood representation of the Trinity: Father, Son and Holy Ghost. She identifies it as the spirit world, though someone else might have other more negative associations to the image of "ghost."

5. Mark: 34–38, Revised English Bible, New Testament, 38.

6. Luke 11:9-10, Revised English Bible, New Testament, 63.

7. In the Christian tradition, the cataphatic (or kataphatic) spiritual way holds that God can be known through God's creation, and through images of God. Thus cataphatic spirituality would include seeing God in God's creation, visions of God, and various mainifestations of God in dreams. The apophatic way, on the other hand, involves the abandonment of all images and concepts of God. It is, to put it in a familiar way, the "way of unknowing." For a full account of cataphatic spirituality, see Harvey D. Egan S.J. "The Affirmative Way," pp. 14–17, in *The New Catholic Dictionary of Spirituality*, ed. Michael Downey (Liturgical Press, Collegeville, Minn. 1993), For a full account of apophatic spirituality see Harvey D. Egan S.J. "The Negative Way, pp. 700–704, ibid.

5. Dreams of Energy

1. General Synod of the Anglican Church, *The Book of Alternative Services* (Toronto: Anglican Book Centre, 1985), 226.

2. General Synod of the Anglican Church, *Book of Alternative Services, 203.*

3. The jaguar makes a particularly good magical animal for Martha, since it is a spirit companion for shamans in the Mayan tradition. It helps the shaman move between the worlds, and in a sense it is what Martha wanted to do, and is trying to do in the dream. There is something powerful and impressive, indeed jaguar-like, about Martha, and something of the shaman as well; she has a powerful and lively presence and the ability to bring about transformation in her life that goes beyond the ordinary. For more about jaguar symbolism in Mesoamerica, see E. P. Benson, "The Lord, the Ruler: Jaguar Symbolism in the Americas" in *Icons of Power: Feline Symbolism in the Americas*, ed. N. J. Saunders (London: Routledge, 1998). Also see M. D. Coe, "Olmec Jaguars and Olmec Kings" in E. P. Benson, ed. *The Cult of the Feline* (Washington D.C.: Dumbarton Oaks, 1999).

4. It might be said that, because Christianity had to do for so long with externally mandated rules and fitting into a system, it is particiularly important to allow both the disorderly activities of the unconscious to come in, and to be able to tolerate a different view of ethics: the mystical point of view, in which paradox and playfulness have a place. A particularly difficult shift for people with very rigid moral views can be the place of the *felix culpa*, the happy fault, the potentially transforming bad thing one does or that happens to one.

5. C. G. Jung, "The Transcendent Function," in *The Structure and Dynamics of the Psyche* (Princeton, N.J.: Princeton University Press, 1960) CW 8.

6. Bad Dreams about the Divine

1. A well-known "bad" vision of the divine, if not a dream, is the vision I describe in the Introduction: Jung's vision of God dropping a turd on the cathedral at Basle. Jung agonized for days, feeling that he was about to have a terrible thought that

would destroy him. When he finally had it, he came feel that it was the occasion of his discovery of the experience of grace, since he would not have had it if it had not been God's will.

2. M. Scott Peck, *The Road Less Traveled* (New York: Simon and Schuster, 1978), 179–80.

3. I would like to thank Everett Ring, a parishioner of St. John the Divine Anglican Church in Victoria, British Columbia, for suggesting this interetesting interpretation of a kind of dream that nearly everyone has had at some time.

4. Søren Kierkegaard, *Concluding Unscientific Postscript to Philosophical Fragments*, ed. and trans. Howard V. Hong and Edna H. Hong (Princeton, N.J.: Princeton University Press, 1992), vol. 1, 311–12.

5. Peck, *Road Less Traveled*, 16–17. This quotation includes a footnote for the quote from Jung: *Collected Works of C. G. Jung*, Bollingen Ser., no. 20, 2nd ed., (Princeton, N.J.: Princeton University Press, 1973), trans. R. F. C. Hull, vol. 11, *Psychology and Religion: West and East*, 75.

6. May, *Will and Spirit*, 6.

7. Jean-Paul Sartre, *Being and Nothingness*, trans. Hazel Barnes (New York: Philosophical Library, 1963), 21.

8. Iris Murdoch, "On 'God' and 'Good'" in *Existentialists and Mystics*, ed. Peter Conradi (New York: The Penguin Press, 1998), 341.

9. It is this kind of consciousness and reflection that Jaspers recommends as an alternative to unconsciousness, literal-mindedness, and/or theorizing in developing our relationships with boundary situations.

10. For an extensive discussion of this interpretation of Job's story, see Edward Edinger, *Transformation of the God Image* (Toronto: Inner City Books, 1992).

11. The dark night of the senses and the dark night of the soul are both stages of purgation on the mystical path of union with God, called the unitive way. The dark night of the senses is a preparation for the birth of the divine in the soul, and the dark night of the soul is a deeper purgation preparatory to union with the divine that occurs after the soul's awakening to the divine. For more detailed discussions of these spiritual stages, see Thomas McGonigle "The Unitive Way" in *The New Dictionary of Catholic Spirituality,* ed. Michael Downey (Collegeville, Minn.: Liturgical Press, 1993); St. John of the Cross, *The Dark Night of the Soul,* trans. with an introd. by E. Allison Peers (New York: Image Books, 1959); Kenneth Leach, *Soul Friend* (San Francisco:, HarperSanfrancisco), 1992), 137–67; Evelyn Underhill, *Mysticism* (New York: Image Books, 1990), 167–443.

7. Tiffany's Transformation

1. For an excellent discussion of this phenomenon, see Mario Jacoby, "Transference and Counter-Transference," in *The Analytic Encounter* (Toronto: Inner City Books, 1984).

2. For a helpful discusioon of both overlap and difference, see Wolff-Salin, "Listening, Silence, Obedience" and "Spiritual Guide or Therapist," in *No Other Light*.

8. Grace's Grace-Filled Journey

1. Sartre, *Being and Nothingness*, 557–615.

2. The pearl of great price is a parable and the widow's mite is a story in the New Testament. The parable of the pearl of great price appears in Matthew 13:45 46, comparing the Kingdom of Heaven to a pearl of great price, something worth selling everything for. The story of the widow's mite appears in Mark 12:42–44. In it, Jesus compares the ostentatious giving of the rich at the temple to a tiny amount given by a widow. He points out that while the rich gave a great deal, they still have more than enough, the widow gave everything she had.

3. A presentation dream is the dream presented to the counselor/therapist/spiritual director at the first session. Many believe it to have special significance for the coming work.

4. Ann Belford Ulanov, *Primary Speech* (Atlanta: Westminster John Knox Press, 1982), 17.

9. Transference and Spiritual Connection

1. For example, many clergy are the recipients of archetypal projections. Their parishioners get them mixed up with God and have more or less the same expectations of clergy that they would of God. Since this is unconscious, the parishioner may eventually become extremely angry with clergy for the inevitable human failures that occur in all relationships and/or the clergyperson may also be unconsciously drawn into the projections and attempt to live out this relationship and exhaust her or himself in the process, and/or the clergyperson with unresolved sexual issues may use this power to exploit the parishioner. These are only a few of the painful possibilities of unconscious archetypal projection.

2. For a useful discussion of the notion of the spiritual mother, see John Layard, "The Two Mothers," in *A Celtic Quest* (Dallas, Tex.: Spring Publications, 1975).

3. Jacoby, *Analytic Encounter*, passim.

4. See Hildegarde of Bingen, *Hildegarde of Bingen: Mystical Writings*, ed. and trans. with commentary by Fiona Bowie and Oliver Davies (New York: Crossroad Spiritual Classics Series, 1990).

5. This dream appears in Bonnelle Lewis Strickling, "Reclaiming the Inner Child," in *Healing Voices*, ed. Toni Ann Laidlaw, Cheryl Malmo, and associates (San Francisco: Jossey-Bass, 1990), 149.

6. See also Grace's dream, "The Living Lake."

7. Philip Hallie, *Lest Innocent Blood Be Shed* (New York: Harper and Row, 1979).

8. And vice versa. My first analyst memorably said to me that not only does the analysand find the analyst she needs, but also the analyst finds the analysand. This has been true over and over in my life. In his essay "The Psychology of the Transference" in *The Practice of Psychotherapy*, 2nd ed. (Princeton, N.J.: Princeton University Press, 1966), CW 16, Jung argues that both analyst and analysand are transformed in the process of psychotherapy, or the process is unsuccessful.

10. Coming Home

1. See, e.g., Rizzuto, *Birth of the Living God.*

2. Jung, *Letters,* Vol. 2, 130. As I mentioned in earlier chapters, extended discussions of the Jungian approach to spiritual life are available in the work of contemporary Jungians such as Lionel Corbett, Edward Edinger, John Dourley, Ann Belford Ulanov, and Janet Dallett. Murray Stein also offers helpful discussions of Jung's relation to Christianity. See Murray Stein, *Jung's Treatment of Christianity* (Wilmette, Ill.: Chiron Publications, 1985).

3. E.g., Edinger, Corbett, and Dallett.

4. A particularly vivid description of church experienced as home in this way occurs in Anne Lamott's book *Traveling Mercies:* "When I was at the end of my rope, the people at St. Andrew tied a knot in it for me and helped me hold on. The church became my home in the old meaning of *home*—that it's where, when you show up, they have to let you in. They let me in. They even said, 'you come back now.'" I want to thank Pat Brand of Memphis for directing me to the work of Anne Lamott. Anne Lamott, *Traveling Mercies* (New York: Anchor Books, 2000), 100.

5. See, e.g., C. G. Jung, "Transformation Symbolism in the Mass" in *Psychology and Religion: West and East* (Princeton, N.J.: Princeton University Press, 1958), CW 11.

6. For further discussion of this point, see Hall, "Religious Images in Dreams," *Unconscious Christian.*

7. For more on the Navajo tradition and the pollen path, see Margaret Schevill Link, *The Pollen Path*, collected Navajo myths with a psychological commentary by Joseph Henderson (Walnut, Ca.: Kiva Publishing, 1998). Also see Joseph Henderson, *Thresholds of Initiation* (Middletown, Conn.: Wesleyan University Press, 1967).

8. T. S. Eliot, *Collected Poems, 1909-1962* (London: Faber and Faber, 1964), 222.

9. E.g. Karl Jaspers's notion of "the loving struggle for Existenz" in *Philosophy,* vol. 2, 212.

10. An example of the difference appears in Mary's Magnificant, in which she moves from accepting her fate to welcoming it.

11. Gary Snyder, *Earth House Hold* (New York: New Directions, 1957), 39.

12. In fact, in an earlier work, *General Psychopathology* (Chicago: University of Chicago Press and Manchester University Press, 1963), Jaspers expressed a strong disagreement with Jung's views about archetypes.

11. Dreams: The Divine Connection

1. Dooley, *Passion for the Impossible.*

2. *Book of Alternative Services,* 214.

Bibliography

Augustine. *Confessions.* Trans. R. S. Pine-Coffin. Harmondsworth: Penguin, 1961.

Benson, E. P., ed. *The Cult of the Feline.* Washington, D.C.: Dumbarton Oaks, 1999.

Brooke, Roger. *Jung and Phenomenology.* Routledge: London, 1991.

Bulkeley, Kelly. *The Wilderness of Dreams.* Albany: State University of New York Press, 1994.

Copleston, F. C. *A History of Philosophy,* vols. 1–9. New York: Image Books, vols. 1–6 , 1993; vols. 7–9, 1994.

Corbett, Lionel. *The Religious Function of the Psyche.* London: Routledge, 1996.

Dallett, Janet. *The Not-Yet-Transformed God.* York Beach, Me.: Nicolas-Hays, 1998.

———. *When the Spirits Come Back.* Toronto: Inner City Books, 1988.

de Beauvoir, Simone. *The Ethics of Ambiguity.* Trans. Bernard Frechtman. 7th ed. Secaucus, N.J.: Citadel Press, 1975.

Dooley, Mark, ed. *A Passion for the Impossible.* Albany: State University of New York Press, 2003.

Dourley, John. *Love, Celibacy, and the Inner Marriage.* Toronto: Inner City Books, 1987.

———. *A Strategy for the Loss of Faith.* Toronto: Inner City Books, 1992.

Downey, Michael, ed. *The New Dictionary of Catholic Spirituality.* Collegeville, Minn.: Liturgical Press, 1993.

Edinger, Edward. *The Creation of Consciousness*. Toronto: Inner City Books, 1984.

———. *The Transformation of the God Image*. Toronto: Inner City Books, 1992.

Eigen, Michael. *The Psychoanalytic Mystic*. Binghamton: esf Publications, 1998.

Eliot, T. S. *Collected Poems, 1909-1962*. London: Faber and Faber, 1964.

Freud, Sigmund. "The Uncanny" in *The Uncanny*. Trans. David McClintock with an introduction by Hugh Haughton. New York: Penguin, 2003.

General Synod of the Anglican Church. *Book of Alternative Services*. Toronto: Anglican Book Centre, 1985.

———. *Book of Common Prayer*. Toronto: Anglican Book Centre, 1962.

Giegerich, Wolfgang. *The Soul's Logical Life*. Frankfurt: Peter Lang, 2001.

Hall, James. *The Unconscious Christian*. Mahwah, N.J.: Paulist Press, 1993.

Hallie, Philip. *Lest Innocent Blood Be Shed*. New York: Harper and Row, 1979.

Henderson, Joseph. *Thresholds of Initiation*. Middletown, Conn.: 1967.

Hildegarde of Bingen. *Hildegarde of Bingen: Mystical Writings*. Ed. and trans. with commentary by Fiona Bowie and Oliver Davies. New York: Crossroads Spiritual Classics Series, 1990.

Jacoby, Mario. *The Analytic Encounter*. Toronto: Inner City Books, 1984.

Jaspers, Karl. *General Psychopathology*. Chicago: University of Chicago Press, 1963.

———. *Philosophy*, vol. 2. Trans. E. B. Ashton. Chicago: University of Chicago Press, 1970.

John of the Cross, St. *The Dark Night of the Soul*. Trans. and with intro. by E. Allison Peers. New York: Image Books, 1959.

Julian of Norwich. *Julian of Norwich: Showings*. Trans. Edward Colledge O. S. A. and James Walsh S. J. New York: Paulist Press, 1978.

Jung, C. G. *Letters*, vol. 2. Ed. G. Adler and A. Jaffe. Trans. R. F. C. Hull. Princeton: Princeton University Press, 1954.

———. *Memories, Dreams, and Reflections*. New York: Vintage Books, 1989.

————. *The Practice of Psychotherapy*. 2nd ed. CW 16. Princeton: Princeton University Press, 1966.

————. *Psychology and Religion*. CW 11, Princeton: Princeton University Press, 1958.

————. *The Structure and Dynamics of the Psyche*. CW 8. Princeton: Princeton University Press, 1960.

Kelly, Sean. *Individuation and the Absolute*. Mahwah, N.J.: Paulist Press, 1993.

Kierkegaard, Søren. *Concluding Unscientific Postscript to Philosophical Fragments*. Ed. and trans. by Howard V. Hong and Edna H. Hong. Princeton: Princeton University Press, 1992.

Lamott, Anne. *Traveling Mercies*. New York: Anchor Books, 2000.

Layard, John. *A Celtic Quest*. Dallas: Spring Publications, 1975.

Leach, Kenneth. *Soul Friend*. San Francisco: HarperSanFrancisco, 1992.

Link, Margaret Schevill. *The Pollen Path*. Walnut, Cal., 1998.

Long, A. A. *Hellenistic Philosophy*. Berkeley: University of California Press, 2003.

May, Gerald. *Will and Spirit*. San Francisco: HarperSanfrancisco, 1987.

Miller, Alice. *The Drama of the Gifted Child*. New York: Basic Books/Harper Collins, 1981.

Murdoch, Iris. *An Accidental Man*. London: Chatto and Windus, 1971.

————. *Existentialists and Mystics*. Ed. Peter Conradi. New York: Allen Lane, Penguin Press, 1998.

————. *A Fairly Honourable Defeat*. London: Chatto and Windus, 1970.

————. *The Nice and the Good*. London: Chatto and Windus, 1968.

————. *Nuns and Soldiers*. London: Chatto and Windus, 1980.

Nagy, Marilyn. *Philosophical Issues in the Psychology of C. G. Jung*. Albany: State University of New York Press, 1991.

Peck, M. Scott. *The Road Less Traveled*. New York: Simon and Schuster, 1978.

Pietikainen, Petteri. *C. G. Jung and the Psychology of Symbolic Forms*. Helsinki: Annales Academiae Scientiarum Fennicae, 1999.

Revised English Bible. Oxford: Oxford University Press and Cambridge University Press, 1989.

Ricoeur, Paul. *Freedom and Nature: The Voluntary and the Involuntary.* Trans. Erazim Kohak. Evanston: Northwestern University Press, 1966.

Rizzuto, Ana-Maria. *The Birth of the Living God.* Chicago: University of Chicago Press, 1979.

Salamun, Kurt. "Jaspers." In *A Companion to Continental Philosophy*, ed. Simon Critchley and Schroeder, William R. Malden, Mass.: Blackwells, 1998.

Sartre, Jean-Paul. *Being and Nothingness.* Trans. Hazel Barnes. New York: Philosophical Library, 1963.

Saunders, N. J. *Icons of Power: Feline Symbolism in the Americas.* London: Routledge, 1998.

Snyder, Gary. *Earth House Hold.* New York: New Directions, 1957.

Stein, Murray. *Jung's Treatment of Christianity.* Wilmette, Ill.: Chiron Publications, 1985.

Strickling, Bonnelle Lewis. "Reclaiming the Inner Child." In *Healing Voices*, ed. Toni Ann Laidlaw, Cheryl Malmo, and associates. San Francisco: Jossey-Bass, 1990.

Ulanov, Ann Belford. *Finding Space.* Louisville, Ky.: Westminster John Knox Press, 2001.

———. *The Functioning Transcendent.* Wilmette, Ill.: Chiron Publications, 1996.

———. *Primary Speech.* Atlanta: Westminster John Knox Press, 1982.

Underhill, Evelyn. *Mysticism.* New York: Image Books, 1990.

Wolff-Salin, Mary. *No Other Light.* New York: Crossroads Press, 1986.

Wollheim, Richard. *On the Emotions.* New Haven: Yale University Press, 1999.

Index